GARLAND STUDIES ON

# ENTREPRENEURSHIP

*edited by*

STUART BRUCHEY
ALLAN NEVINS PROFESSOR EMERITUS
COLUMBIA UNIVERSITY

A GARLAND SERIES

# ENTREPRENEURIAL TEAMS AS DETERMINANTS OF NEW VENTURE PERFORMANCE

MICHAEL D. ENSLEY

GARLAND PUBLISHING, Inc.
A MEMBER OF THE TAYLOR & FRANCIS GROUP
NEW YORK & LONDON / 1999

Published in 1999 by
Garland Publishing Inc.
A Member of the Taylor & Francis Group
19 Union Square West
New York, NY 10003

10 9 8 7 6 5 4 3 2 1

**Library of Congress Cataloging-in-Publication Data**
Ensley, Michael D., 1965–
    Entrepreneurial teams as determinants of new venture performance /
Michael D. Ensley.
        p.   cm — (Garland studies in entrepreneurship)
    Originally presented as the author's doctoral thesis.
    Includes bibliographical references and index.
    ISBN 0-8153-3509-1 (alk. paper)
    1. New business enterprises.   2. Entrepreneurship.   3. New
business enterprises—Econometric models.   4. Entrepreneurship—
mathematical models.   I. Title.   II. Series.
HD62.5.E558   1999
338'.04—dc21                                                    99-29109
                                                                      CIP

Printed on acid-free, 250-year-life paper
Manufactured in the United States of America

I would like to dedicate this research to my wife, Courtney Anne, my parents, Haven and Pauline Ensley, and my mentors Jim and Jo Ann Carland. My wife for her love, warmth, and dedication. My mother for her unwavering belief in me. Belief that has stood the test of time. My father for his devotion to his son. A more loving, caring, and compassionate man I have never known. He demonstrated to me the entrepreneurial spirit. Finally, my mentors for their ability to see what was not there and to help me catch the dream.

# Contents

# Preface

Research that attempts to understand the determinants of new venture performance are not new. There are forty studies that are cited in this book related to the concept of new venture performance. The field of Entrepreneurship has a legacy of working to support practitioners. It is in many ways an applied field. The development of comprehensive new venture performance models is clearly a major step in the construction of a bridge between theorists and practitioners in entrepreneurship.

While new venture performance as a concept is not new the reality is that multi-variate models that are as complicated as the new venture creation process might infer are relatively new. The first major work on a multi-variate new venture performance model was not published until 1986. The inherent complexity of the new venture creation process not withstanding, modeling of new venture performance has continued to be simplistic. Two main variables have been found and have dominated past new venture performance research. These variables are new venture strategy and industry structure. This left the creator of the firm out of the model completely. The creator was deemed to have no significant effect on new venture performance.

The decision to leave the entrepreneur out of the new venture performance model was certainly one that should have not been made in haste. It appears that the decision was made more expediently than necessary. Basically, Sandberg's small sample of sixteen firms justified dropping the entrepreneur from the new venture performance model. Even Sandberg warned of such a hasty conclusion to eliminate the entrepreneur. Though it became one of my missions to set the record straight, I feared that proposing the capture and measurement of the entrepreneur in the same way would not be acceptable. This led to my proposal that the behaviors and dynamics of the new venture team could be among the factors that determine the performance of the new venture. To this end, three literature streams were synthesized for a theoretical base. Empirical work was conducted with *inc. 500* firms that should be more likely to be team managed and driven.

The innovativeness of the study however would have to go beyond the addition of new venture teams. Since there was a tradition of new venture performance research other innovations would have to be added as well. One of those innovations was a profound concentration on measurement and reliability and validity that had alluded most entrepreneurship researchers.

We in entrepreneurship have an awesome task that appears to be growing daily; to assure that the current growth oriented entrepreneurial economy survives for sometime into the future. At the least we as scientists need to understand the entrepreneurial process so that practitioners can learn from their own insight. It is the foundation on which our future success will be laid. It is clear that the complex process of new venture creation and performance are complex. Models that contain only two or three variables are unlikely to make substantial contributions to the field. New venture performance researchers may have taken the concept of parsimony a bit too far, having modeled one of the most complex processes of human activity with three variables. The model is simply under-specified.

We must, as a field, correct our past mistakes and build more representative models. Since the process is complex, the models we build should reflect that complexity. This is not to say that the model proposed in this book is fully specified. However, I feel that it is more fully specified than most proposed in the past and far most explanatory than models with only strategy and industry structure as independent variables. As I do at the end, I will invite you now to join me in the effort to more fully specify the new venture performance model. Let's revise it on the grounds of sound reasoning and empirical support. For the field of entrepreneurship to survive over the long-term, it is important that multiple sample decisions be made on substantive issues. Eliminating entrepreneurs from new venture performance research does not exemplify such reason and thought. The message is simple: let's follow the behavior of entrepreneurs and see if their behavior changes the speed of firm growth and ability to generate sizable cash streams. That is, after all, why they showed up. Enjoy.

*Michael D. Ensley*

# Acknowledgments

There are so many people to thank for my survival of this process. Dr. Garry Smith, who saved me from doom several times throughout my doctoral program. He is a true friend and his efforts will never be forgotten. Thanks to Dr. Allison Harrison to whom I feel a permeant personal bond. She has pushed me and been a friend at the same time. Thanks to Dr. McRae Banks who started this journey with me and made a lasting impression on me. The talents I gained from him will not be forgotten. Thanks to Dr. Ronald Taylor and Dr. Charles Campbell who were selfless members of my dissertation committee. Thanks to Dr. Mark Sharfman whose guidance on the measurement of the environment was indispensable. Thanks to Pinks Dudley whose editing elevated my writing significantly through this process. Most importantly, I would like to thank my dissertation chair, Dr. Barbara A. Spencer, for her guidance throughout this process. Dr. Spencer and I developed a great mentoring relationship for which I will be forever grateful. Dr. Spencer invests herself in her students and I will be forever changed because of her investment in me. Finally, the author wishes to thank the Center for Entrepreneurial Leadership Inc. at the Ewing Marion Kauffman Foundation for their financial support of this project. Dr. Donald Sexton was particularly understanding during this process.

# Tables and Figures

# ENTREPRENEURIAL TEAMS AS DETERMINANTS OF NEW VENTURE PERFORMANCE

# CHAPTER 1
# Introduction

In a recent article entitled "Finding the Entrepreneur in Entrepreneurship," Gartner, Shaver, Gatewood, & Katz (1994) argue that the "entrepreneur in entrepreneurship" is more likely to be plural than singular. That is, entrepreneurial firms are more likely to be started by teams of entrepreneurs than individual entrepreneurs. This goes against the belief long held by many researchers in the field of entrepreneurship that most entrepreneurial firms are started by individuals (Gartner, 1988; Carland, Hoy, Boulton & Carland, 1984). Gartner and his colleagues (1994) suggest that viewing entrepreneurship as a collective activity, rather than an individual one, is a new meta-theme that has remained basically unexplored either conceptually or empirically. Moreover, little is known about the effect of team level behaviors on the development of organizational strategy and new venture performance. It is the purpose of this study to explore the effect of entrepreneurial team behavior on both organizational strategy and new venture performance.

This chapter is arranged in the following manner. The first section addresses the question: are entrepreneurial firms different from established firms? The question is important because it deals with the reasons entrepreneurial firms must be studied as a separate set of organizations from those currently being examined by strategic management researchers in the top management teams area. The second section addresses the importance of entrepreneurial firms in economic development and the importance of this study in particular. It outlines the current state of new venture performance research and describes the important advances in this area. The third section justifies the study of entrepreneurial teams as opposed to individual entrepreneurs and explains how entrepreneurial teams contribute to new venture performance by developing and implementing strategic decisions that match the demands of the industry and environment. The final section lists the research questions addressed by this study, summarizes the chapter, and outlines the remainder of the dissertation.

## ARE ENTREPRENEURIAL FIRMS DIFFERENT FROM ESTABLISHED FIRMS?

Two basic assumptions exist in almost all research on entrepreneurial firms. The first is that entrepreneurial firms are valuable to society and aid economic development. The second major assumption is possibly even more basic than the first; it is that entrepreneurial firms are different from established business organizations. This section explores some conceptual evidence supporting this distinction.

Gartner, Bird, and Starr (1992) distinguish between organizational behavior in established firms versus entrepreneurial behavior in emerging firms. They argue that the difference between the behaviors of the two types of firms are quantum. Miller and Friesen's (1984) *quantum theory of organizational change* can help explain this point. Basically, the theory states that an organization's existence is characterized by periods of calm followed by short periods of dramatic strategic revolution and then basic periods of calm again (Mintzberg, 1987). The periods of calm can be characterized as time spent achieving organizational "simplicity" (Miller, 1993) such as when the organization pursues one specific strategy. During this period of time spent achieving "simplicity" the organization comes to create a particular organizational "Gestalt" (Miller and Friesen, 1984). Emerging organizations have experienced no revolutions, nor have they had time to develop an organizational "Gestalt." Because of this, emerging and established organizations have fundamentally different reactions to the behaviors of their organizational members. Notably, the managerial behaviors observed in both types of organizations might well be the same, but the effects of these behaviors on organizational variables like strategy and new venture performance could be markedly different.

Gartner and his colleagues (1992) argue that entrepreneurial organizations are bound in "an equivocal reality" (p. 16) whereas established firms exist in a "nonequivocal reality." In the established firm, the organizational culture is already developed. Because the values and basic assumptions of those within the culture are established (Schein, 1985), members share common reactions to certain kinds of behaviors. Over time, these reactions become fairly predictable.

In contrast, outcomes of behaviors and events in the equivocal entrepreneurial firms can only be guessed, because a system of values and basic assumptions about the world in which the firm exists has yet to be created. Entrepreneurial teams must enact their reality and create the interactions in their firms because this is the first time that certain behaviors have occurred. Predicting the outcomes of certain behaviors within the team is much more difficult than making similar predictions in established firms where the organizational culture is set. This distinction is the principle difference between established and entrepreneurial firms.

The difference between established and entrepreneurial firms is not one of degree; it is one of quantum proportion. Bygrave (1989a,b) supports this point when he argues that the act of entrepreneurship is discontinuous. The entrepreneurial event breaks with normal business operations and can create a new way of doing business. These new businesses are different both in terms of how they operate and why they choose to operate. Bygrave argues that entrepreneurship is a science of turbulence and change not continuity. The traditional links between the behaviors of the organizational actors and organizational variables such as strategy and performance cannot be assumed. These quantum differences have important implications for this study in that the team dynamics variables studied may lead to different outcomes than might be expected among teams from a sample of established firms. As Gartner et al. (1992) note, many of the behaviors found in established firms do exist in entrepreneurial firms. But how those behaviors link with team effectiveness, strategic choice, and organizational performance, may well be radically different.

## So Differences Exist, Do They Really Matter?

This study is based on the assumption that quantum differences exist between entrepreneurial and established firms. But are entrepreneurial firms really important enough to warrant separate study? If they are important, are the team dynamics, which are the emphasis of this study, important to overall entrepreneurial firm performance?

There is some evidence that entrepreneurial firms are important. Both Kirzner (1979) and Schumpeter (1942) identify entrepreneurial firms as the key to economic activity. According to Kirzner and Schumpeter, entrepreneurs drive economies toward or from economic disequilibrium. Both argue that entrepreneurship is the source of innovation and wealth creation in capitalistic economies.

The Small Business Administration's *Report of the President* noted that for the years 1965 to 1985, 35 million new jobs were created in the U.S. by business and government. If we categorize job growth into job growth by government, large businesses, and medium and small businesses, the findings demonstrate that all of the new jobs created in the U.S. during this period were created by small and medium size firms. Governments saw no change in employment numbers during the 1965-1985 period. Large businesses or corporations saw approximately 5 million jobs cut from their payrolls. Medium and small firms in contrast created an impressive 40 million new jobs (Drucker, 1985). Herron (1990) argued that new ventures not only drive the current economy but also keeps the United States globally competitive.

The importance of the present study is that it attempts to link behaviors and actions of entrepreneurial teams to business strategy and new venture performance. Tests of some of these links have already been conducted in established firms. Yet the quantum differences between established and entrepreneurial firms should theoretically cause some differences in the links between certain behavioral variables at the team level and firm level variables such as strategy and firm performance. This study begins the testing process in entrepreneurial organizations.

## Definitions of Terms Unique to This Study

This short section contains a short definition for each of the terms which are unique to this study. A more detailed definition is presented in Chapter Three.

Entrepreneurial team: A person is classified into an entrepreneurial team if they have two of the three following qualities: founder status, involvement in strategic decisions, and/or owners of 10 percent of the firm (Kamm et al., 1990; Ensley and Banks, 1992).

Entrepreneurial team skill heterogeneity is defined as the total difference between all members' skills (Roure and Madique, 1986; Herron, 1990; Katz, 1974).

Cognitive conflict is defined as frustration directed at ideas (Amason, 1996; Jehn, 1992).

Affective conflict is defined as emotion or frustration directed towards people (Amason, 1996; Jehn, 1992).

Strategic orientation is defined as the characteristics of a new venture's strategic choice (Venkatraman, 1989).

Riskiness is defined as the amount of risk to which strategic actions expose firm resources (Miller and Friesen, 1982, 1983).

Aggressiveness is the extent to which the firm's strategy attempts to increase market share (Miller and Camp, 1985).

Analysis is defined as the overall problem solving posture of the firm (Venkatraman, 1989).

Futurity is defined as the extent to which new ventures work toward a desired future (Miller and Friesen, 1982, 1983).

Proactiveness is the extent to which the new venture's strategy is pre-emptive to competition (Miller, 1983).

Environment is the domain outside the bounds of the organization (Aldrich, 1979; Dess and Beard, 1984; Sharfman and Dean, 1991).

Dynamism is the level of predictability of environmental change (Aldrich, 1979; Dess and Beard, 1984).

Competitive threat involves the available resources in the new venture's industry environment and the competition for those resources (Sharfman and Dean, 1991).

Complexity is defined as the technological intricacy, market diversity, and geographic concentration of the industry environment (Aldrich, 1979; Dess and Beard, 1984).

Performance is defined as the ability to create wealth (Carland et al., 1984; Gartner, 1985).

## MODELS OF NEW VENTURE PERFORMANCE

Several models of entrepreneurial firm performance exist within the field of entrepreneurship. Most studies have attempted to link certain variables, such as business level strategy and industry structure, to new venture performance. The following section discusses the elements often included in the new venture performance models. The sections also contain suggestions for the expansion of the entrepreneurship paradigm. Appendix A contains a table which describes studies of new venture performance thus far.

### What Is Known About the Factors Which Affect Entrepreneurial Firm Performance?

This research project is based on two studies of new venture performance. The first of these is Sandberg's (1986) linear model of new venture performance, in which new venture performance is the dependent variable. The key independent variables are the characteristics of the entrepreneur, the structure of the industry, and the firm's business level strategy.

Sandberg's model is stated as:

$$NVP = f(E, IS, S)$$

Where NVP is equal to new venture performance, E is equal to the characteristics of the entrepreneur, IS is equal to industry structure, and S is equal to strategy.

In his study, Sandberg finds that industry structure and business strategy are important to new venture performance but he is unable empirically to link the characteristics of the entrepreneur to new venture performance. Sandberg notes that this finding is troubling because most new venture research has centered on new venture performance as a function of the entrepreneur (see Brockhaus, 1980; Carland et al., 1984; and Katz & Gartner, 1988). Despite this finding, Sandberg is unwilling to delete the characteristics of the entrepreneur from the model because venture capitalists tend to value factors specific to the entrepreneur, such as management competence and industry experience, as the most important criteria in funding decisions.

This research project builds on Sandberg's model, by improving the methodologies employed, and reconceptualizing the model (Appendix A outlines the findings of several new venture studies on the factors that influence new venture performance). Sandberg conceptualized the "E" in the new venture performance model at the individual level and measured the characteristics of the individual. In this study the "E" is conceptualized at the team level.

McDougall (1987), and McDougall, Robinson and DeNisi's (1992) new venture performance model explains a great deal of the variance in new venture performance but does not include dimensions attributed directly to the entrepreneur. This model is expressed:

$$NVP = f(O, S, IS, S \times IS)$$

Where NVP is equal to new venture performance, O is equal to the origin of the venture, S is equal to strategy, IS is equal to industry structure, and S x IS is equal to strategy and structure interactions.

McDougall et al's study adds to the body of work on new venture performance by arguing not only that industry structure is important but that the fit or interaction of strategy and environment is important to new venture performance. In fact, a great deal of the new venture performance research tends to support the proposition that new venture success is dependent on business strategy and industry structure (Cooper, Willard & Woo, 1986; Miller & Camp, 1985; Biggadike, 1979; ) as opposed to the characteristics of the entrepreneur. The interaction of strategy and environment is an important addition to the new venture performance model and is accounted for in this study.

In contrast to the work of those who would take the entrepreneur out of the new venture performance model, recent research efforts have attempted to put the entrepreneur back into the model. Herron (1990), for instance, argues that many of the findings of the research cited above and listed in Appendix A can be traced to methodological phenomena and therefore represent statistical anomalies. He argues that the lack of a necessary set of validated scales for construct measurement of entrepreneurial characteristics greatly hampers research in this area. Chandler and Hanks (1994) demonstrate empirically that environment and the competence and experience of the entrepreneur as they relate to strategic choice have a direct effect on new venture performance. Simply, the way that the entrepreneur affects the performance of new ventures is through strategic choice. They argue that, from a strategic choice perspective, the entrepreneur chooses a particular strategy when choice is the greatest, when the firm is new. Previous strategic choices cannot constrain strategic choice when no prior strategic choice has been made. Entrepreneurs make a difference because they use their experiences, competencies, and background to choose business strategy and organizational environment (Weick, 1979). In the same vein, Gartner et al. (1994) argue that the problem with research such as Sandberg's (1986) is that the entrepreneur is misunderstood and misspecified. The entrepreneur's ability to think and understand is important to new venture performance because thinking and understanding are the basis of strategic choice (Child, 1972).

The purpose of this study is to develop further both the conceptual and empirical understanding of the "E" or entrepreneur in Sandberg's (1986) new venture performance model by redefining the individual entrepreneur as an entrepreneurial team. The redefinition of the entrepreneur as a team rather than an individual is consistent with one of the meta-themes outlined by Gartner et al. (1994). It builds on Chandler and Hanks (1994) work by allowing examination of how certain team level behaviors affect strategic choice. Additionally, this research draws on McDougall's (1987) findings to improve the conception of the role of the environment and to incorporate the interactions between strategy and environment. As a result, the new venture performance model proposed in this study can be stated as follows:

$$NVP = f(ET, S, IS, S \times IS)$$

Where NVP is equal to new venture performance, ET is equal to the behaviors, actions, and state of the entrepreneurial team, S is equal to strategy, IS is equal to industry structure, and S x IS is equal to the interaction of the strategy and industry structure.

## HOW DO ENTREPRENEURIAL TEAMS AFFECT NEW VENTURE PERFORMANCE?

A great deal of evidence exists which supports the idea that the entrepreneurial event is most often precipitated by a team of entrepreneurs rather than an individual entrepreneur. Kamm et al. (1990) define entrepreneurial teams as "two or more individuals who jointly establish a firm in which they have a financial interest" (p. 7). Ensley and Banks (1992) and Gartner et al. (1994) extend this definition to include those individuals who have direct influence on strategic choice. For the purposes of this study, an individual who meets two of these three criteria is considered part of the entrepreneurial team.

In an effort to understand the entrepreneurial team and its possible effect on new venture performance, three dimensions of team behavior are examined. These dimensions are team skill heterogeneity, affective conflict, and cognitive conflict. These phenomena are discussed regularly in top management team research and are expected to exist in entrepreneurial firms. Established and entrepreneurial firms differ in the way that such team level behaviors affect organizational outcomes such as strategy and new venture performance (Gartner et al., 1992). In this research, an attempt will be made to link these dimensions theoretically and empirically to strategy, industry structure, the strategy-industry interaction, and performance.

For instance, when top management team members consider a higher number of strategic alternatives they increase the likelihood that cognitive conflict occurs (Amason and Schwiger, 1994). The researcher argues in Chapter Two that cognitive conflict has a positive effect on strategic choice. Considering larger numbers of alternatives, and giving them more thought should lead to better choices about strategy. The existence of cognitive conflict in the entrepreneurial team should positively affect the team's choice of strategy.

Affective conflict has been an issue in organizational behavior for some time (Cosier, 1978) and in educational psychology for an even longer period of time (Achilles, 1992; Cueto, 1993; Hinitz, 1995). Jehn (1992) concludes that affective conflict or social or personality conflict is a type of conflict which causes problems in decision making processes. Amason and Schwiger (1994) argue that strategic decisions are adversely affected by high levels of affective conflict. The abilities of team members to "get along" is an important aspect of both strategic choice, and implementation. Affective conflict within the entrepreneurial team should cause problems with both strategic decision making processes and the implementation of those strategic decisions.

Much of the anecdotal evidence on entrepreneurial teams has concerned the skills of the team members (Roure and Madique, 1986). Roure and Madique argue that entrepreneurial teams which have a skill composition that is more diverse make strategic choices that improve new venture performance. Little is known about the specifics of what configurations work best, but it is clear from their anecdotal work that diverse skills seem to lead to better strategic choices.

The abilities of entrepreneurial team members, their adeptness at getting along with each other, their common experiences, and their understanding of the various strategic challenges which face the firm are all factors which could affect new venture performance. The ability of an entrepreneurial team simply to get along could influence the team's commitment to a new venture and its consensus about how to make it work. Choosing among a whole range of strategic choices, a process that inevitably produces cognitive conflict, would certainly be better than pursuing the same strategy for endless periods without considering alternative strategies (Mintzberg, 1987; Miller, 1993). An entrepreneurial team whose members possess a diverse group of skills should be better able to handle the many diverse and chaotic situations which new ventures face.

Earlier, the works of Bygrave (1989a,b) Gartner et al. (1992), and Miller & Friesen (1984) are cited to demonstrate that entrepreneurial firms are not small established firms; rather, they are radically different. Gartner and his colleagues (1992) argue that this difference in type of firm does not cause a difference in the observable behaviors themselves but that it creates differences in the links between the behaviors and organizational outcomes. The links between the team level behaviors (i.e., affective and cognitive conflict) and team make-up (i.e., skill hetero-geneity) with business level strategy and firm performance are the focus of this study. By determining how these team behaviors influence busi-ness level strategy and new venture performance, it may be possible to expand the new venture performance model. Including entrepreneurial team behaviors, actions, and states of being as opposed to the traits and characteristics of the individual entrepreneur is an intuitively appealing and theoretically justified extension of the entrepreneurship paradigm.

## The Strategy and Performance Relationship

The attempt to link certain strategies to performance has long been the objective of many strategic management researchers. Child (1972) argues that managers have choices about strategy and that those strate-gies affect firm performance. Rumelt (1986) argues that the strategic groups research stream offers the best opportunity for improvement of the understanding of the strategy-performance relationship. He believes that grouping firms with similar strategies enables researchers to see per-formance differences between certain groups of firms and therefore between certain strategies. Even in Mintzberg's (1994) critical writings on the rise and fall of strategic planning, he is clear that strategic thinking and strategic actions influence the performance of organizations.

The link between strategy and performance in new ventures is quite well documented. Appendix A includes several articles that through either anecdotal evidence or statistical models conclude that strategy affects the performance of new ventures. In fact only one of the articles does not list strategy as a variable affecting new venture performance. Sandberg (1986) finds that strategy and industry have direct effects on new venture performance. McDougall et al. (1992) find that strategy alone or strategy interacting with industry structure has a direct influence on the performance of new ventures. In a recent article, Stearns, Carter, Reynolds and Williams (1995) support McDougall's findings. It is clear that strategy does have a "positive" effect on new venture performance but what is the nature or characteristics of the strategy(s) that influence new venture performance?

An answer to this question comes from Miller and Friesen's (1982) comparison of the strategic characteristics of innovative and growing emergent firms with conservative, non-entrepreneurial firms. They viewed strategy as varying from a conservative to an entrepreneurial ori-entation. Miller and Friesen (1982) conclude that entrepreneurial strate-gies are correlated with higher levels of firm growth. Using the same measurement scale Covin (1991) arrived at similar conclusions. They and other researchers characterize an entrepreneurial strategic orientation as Risky (Miller, 1983); Aggressive (Miller and Camp, 1985); Analytical (Miller and Friesen, 1983); Proactive (Miller, 1983 and Miller and Friesen, 1983); and high in Futurity or future oriented (Miller and Friesen, 1983 and Covin 1991). Miller and Friesen (1983), Covin and Slevin, (1989), Covin (1991), and Miller and Camp (1985) all argue that a successful entrepreneurial firm pursues strategies which have the characteristics listed above. Based on these studies, it is assumed in this research that among emerging firms, the pursuit of a more entrepreneurial strategic orientation should lead to improved firm performance. Theoretically, firms should focus on an entrepreneurial strategic orientation for greater firm success (Miller and Friesen, 1982; Miller and Friesen, 1983; Miller, 1983 and Covin, 1991).

## The Strategy-Organizational Task Environment Interaction

The inclusion of the strategy-industry interaction in the new venture performance model, or controlling for industry effects, is an important aspect of strategic management research. Certainly there is theoretical support to include the strategy-industry interaction in new venture research (Bain, 1956; Caves and Porter, 1977; Harrigan, 1981; Porter, 1980; Yip, 1982) yet few researchers have done so with any real methodological rigor (Sandberg, 1986; McDougall, 1987 are exceptions to this). The industrial organizational economics researchers like Bain (1956) and Porter (1980) argue that the structure of the industry plays a key role in the performance of new ventures or any type of firm. Dess, Ireland, and Hitt (1990) argue that without proper controls for industry effects, strategic management research loses credibility, reliability, and validity. Sharfman and Dean (1991) and Dess and Rasheed (1991) echo this conclusion, although they don't agree on the best way to control for industry effects or measure the environment.

Current research tells us little about how the strategy of the new venture and the environment interact. What is the nature of the interactions? Given that new ventures seem to perform better with entrepreneurial strategic orientations rather than conservative ones what types of environments best fit entrepreneurial strategic orientations? Covin and Slevin (1989) conclude that entrepreneurial strategic orientations are successful in hostile environments. Merz and Sauber (1995) link success in new ventures to the match of entrepreneurial strategic orientations and dynamic, hostile and heterogenous industries. Miller and Friesen (1983) link dynamic, hostile, and heterogenous environments with an entrepreneurial strategic orientation for firm success. Based on these studies, one can conclude that new venture performance is affected by the interaction of the new venture's environment and strategic orientation. One would expect positive interactions between strategies which are highly entrepreneurial and environments which are highly dynamic and complex.

The following sections outline the research questions connected with the preceding discussions. Five research questions are offered concerning skill heterogeneity, team behaviors, strategy, environment, and performance. The conclusion of this chapter provides an outline of the remainder of the dissertation.

## RESEARCH QUESTIONS

Of the relationships in the model in Figure One, no one path between dimensions is more tenuous than the relationship between skill heterogeneity and the two types of conflict. Intuitively, skill heterogeneity should increase the levels of both types of conflict. For example, team members with vastly different skills may tend to view problems and solutions to those problems in vastly different ways (Murray, 1989). This would raise the level of cognitive conflict. Several articles imply that this might be true within established firms (Bantel and Jackson, 1989; Jackson et al., 1991). The demography researchers in the top management team (cf., Hambrick, 1993; Michel and Hambrick, 1992; Pfeffer and Salancik, 1978) area argue that team diversity improves the performance of the executive team by increasing the number of perspectives and possible alternatives considered by the team when considering strategic decisions (Jackson et al., 1991; Wiersema & Bird, 1993).

Other studies find the negative effects of team diversity. For instance top management team turnover is increased by team heterogeneity. Jackson et al. (1991) imply that this link applies to skill heterogeneity as measured by college degree, major in college, and type of functional position. One of the reasons for the shorter team tenure of those who are different, have a different set of demographic characteristics or set of skills, might be the level of affective conflict which exists within the team. Kabanoff (1991) argues that individual differences raise the level of affective conflict. Gladstein's (1984) model of group behavior posed a direct link to the level of conflict and therefore to the discussion of strategy. She also argues that a relationship exists between the skill composition of the group and firm performance.

None of the studies in this review measure the actual skills of team members. Most often, some functionally oriented surrogate, such as major in college and present functional area is used. This methodological shortfall and the lack of conflict research without skill heterogeneity measures make this hypothesis difficult to develop and more exploratory than most of the hypotheses in this study. In this study, Bollen's (1989) theoretical development arguments serve as a guide. Bollen suggests that path models should follow intuitively appealing paths when the area lacks specific conceptual guidance. Therefore, the first research question is:

*Research Question One: How does skill heterogeneity affect the level of affective and cognitive conflict in entrepreneurial teams?*

To date, few studies of team level conflict in entrepreneurial firms are complete. Research by Eisenhardt and Bourgeois (1988) is one exception. Eisenhardt and Bourgeois (1988) demonstrate that the existence of high levels of affective conflict in high velocity, entrepreneurial firms has no influence on entrepreneurial team cooperation levels or firm performance. This finding differs from the case of established firms where affective conflict in top management teams is thought to be debilitating to strategic decision making (Schweiger, Sandberg, Ragan 1986). Eisenhardt and Bourgeois (1988) explain this discrepancy by showing some empirical evidence which supports the notion that affective conflict has no effect on firm performance because of the fear of firm death.

Although they did not specifically study cognitive conflict in entrepreneurial teams, Eisenhardt's (1989) qualitative study and Eisenhardt and Schoonhoven's (1990) empirical study imply that cognitive conflict has a positive influence on the performance of entrepreneurial firms. The conclusion of both studies is that better decisions by entrepreneurial teams are made by teams that consider the greatest number of alternatives and utilized the greatest amount of information. The greater the number of alternatives considered the higher the level of cognitive conflict (Amason, 1996; Schweiger et al., 1989). It seems likely that by considering more alternatives and enduring more cognitive conflict that entrepreneurial teams make better choices about business level strategy. Thus, the following research question is offered:

*Research Question Two: How do entrepreneurial team behaviors (i.e. affective and cognitive conflict) affect the choice of business level strategy?*

The relationship between strategy and new venture performance is well documented. Sandberg (1986), McDougall (1987), McDougall et al. (1992), Sterns et al. (1994) all conclude that new venture performance is affected by strategic orientation. Strategy is an important variable in the new venture performance model which has been included since Biggadike's (1976) qualitative study. In the prior paragraph the researcher argues that entrepreneurial teams with high levels of cognitive conflict would choose more appropriate strategies. Following this logic it makes sense that better strategies should enhance firm performance. This leads to the third research question:

> *Research Question Three: Does business level strategy affect new venture performance?*

The effect of the environment on the performance of the firm is well documented (Porter, 1980; Bain, 1956). Industry structure in particular is posed to have an effect on new venture performance (Sandberg, 1986). McDougall (1987) and McDougall et al. (1992) proposed and empirically support a proposition that new venture strategies interact with industry structure to affect performance. This leads to the fourth and fifth research questions:

> *Research Question Four: Does the environment affect the performance of new ventures?*

> *Research Question Five: Does the interaction of environment and strategic orientation affect the performance of new ventures?*

The final research question is oriented or based on a possible direct connection between affective conflict and new venture performance. Cosier (1978) concludes that affective conflict has a direct effect on firm performance by creating a situation in which no one could work as a team. Affective conflict devastates the level of commitment to organizational goals (Amason, 1996). This scant evidence which ties team behaviors to new venture performance prompts the final research question:

> *Research Question Five: Does affective conflict directly affect new venture performance?*

## OUTLINE OF REMAINDER OF DISSERTATION

The remainder of this dissertation contains the theoretical foundation for the development of this study, the research design and methodology, findings, conclusions, and implications. Chapter Two establishes the theoretical foundation for this study through relevant articles from four streams of literature: first, the relevant literature on top management teams from strategic management is reviewed to build a theoretical and conceptual foundation for the study of entrepreneurial teams; second the relevant groups literature from organizational behavior is utilized for its richness and depth concerning the relationships between team level behaviors and firm performance; third, the literature which is specifically related to entrepreneurial teams and entrepreneurial firms is reviewed to provide a better understanding of specific entrepreneurial team behavior and the conceptual linkages which exist between team behaviors and organizational level variables in entrepreneurial firms; fourth, the literature review discusses the link between business level strategy and overall firm performance; finally, literature on the environment is discussed and the strategy-environment interaction and its potential influence on new venture performance. Chapter Three follows with a discussion of the research model, research and sample design, construct measurement and validation, and statistical methods employed. Chapter Four reports the findings of this research and Chapter Five discusses the conclusions and managerial implications of this project.

CHAPTER 2

# Literature Review
# and Theoretical Basis

This chapter will be presented in four sections in an effort to provide theoretical support for the model shown in Appendix B and to develop hypotheses based on the five research questions in chapter one. The first section will develop a theoretical grounding for a possible relationship between skill heterogeneity and conflict in entrepreneurial teams. Research from the top management teams area in strategic management and the groups literature in organizational behavior will be integrated with the scant literature on entrepreneurial teams in attempt to develop such a grounding.

The second section describes the evidence which supports links from cognitive and affective conflict to strategic orientation. Research on top management teams will be reviewed and presented as evidence that cognitive conflict has a positive effect on the strategic orientation of new ventures and the level of affective conflict. Affective conflict while not as conceptually clear as cognitive conflict will be conceptually tied to new venture performance and strategic orientation.

The third section will examine the link between strategic orientation and new venture performance. Strategy and new venture performance have been constant theoretical companions since Sandberg's dissertation in 1986. Several studies will be reviewed which discuss the characteristics of strategy in successful new ventures.

The fourth section will discuss the effect of the industry environment on strategic orientation and new venture performance. A theoretical argument will be made as to why the relationship between strategy and environment in new ventures has traditionally been viewed from a fit perspective. As with previous new venture research, strategic orientation will be thought to interact with the environment to affect the performance of new ventures (McDougall, 1987).

## ESTABLISHING A LINK BETWEEN SKILL HETEROGENEITY, AND AFFECTIVE AND COGNITIVE CONFLICT

Of the many factors which have been studied in the literature on top management teams, two types of team heterogeneity have dominated. The chief focus has been on demographic heterogeneity, defined as demographic differences between team members on characteristics such as national origin, gender, and age (Hambrick, 1993). Top management team skill heterogeneity is also an important research topic (Murray, 1989). Skill heterogeneity has been explored qualitatively and anecdotally by entrepreneurship researchers and found to improve new venture performance.

In addition to the discussions of team heterogeneity, additional research has focused on the role of conflict in the decision-making process. As with heterogeneity, two types of conflict are believed to exist in top management teams: cognitive and affective conflict. These constructs have been investigated in the context of team turnover (Wiersema & Bird, 1993), consensus, agreement, and decision quality (Amason & Schwieger, 1994), and overall firm performance (Norburn & Birley, 1988). In the following section, skill heterogeneity, cognitive conflict, and affective conflict are examined in the context of strategic decision making to discover the current state of knowledge of these issues in established and emerging firms.

### Evidence Linking Skill Heterogeneity to Conflict

Murray (1989) attempted to link top management team heterogeneity to organizational performance. He argued that the more heterogenous the skills or functional backgrounds of top management team members; the better the firm's long-term performance will be. Moreover, he contended that heterogeneity would have positive long-term and negative short-term performance effects. The short-term losses would be associated with the development of relationships between team members. The important point in Murray's study is that over time, higher skill or functional heterogeneity leads to better strategic decisions and therefore better long-term firm performance.

The sample in Murray's study included 84 firms from the oil and food industries in the Fortune 500. His source of data was the Dun and Bradstreet *Reference Book of Corporate Managements.* Murray measured skill heterogeneity as the differences in education, major in highest degree, and occupational or functional background among top management team members.

Murray found that team heterogeneity, based on functional area and educational background, was a significant predictor of long-term firm performance. Top management team factors accounted for about twenty-five percent of the variation in short term performance and over fifty percent of the variation in long-term firm performance. Thus, skill heterogeneity should encourage a better set of alternatives to be considered by the team, and each alternative should be considered at greater depth than it might be in a team with more homogenous skills. Considering greater numbers of alternatives should increase the level of cognitive conflict within the team.

Bantel and Jackson (1989) linked skill heterogeneity and cognitive conflict in a study that examined innovation in banking. The objective of their research was to link the composition of the top management team to innovations in the banking industry. Their sample included top managers from 198 banks in six states. Heterogeneity was operationalized as the difference among team members in tenure, age, functional area, educational level, and major field of study in the highest degree. These differences were assessed by measuring these characteristics for each team member and then calculating the coefficient of variation. Innovation was measured in a manner similar to Daft's (1978) industry specific measures of innovation. Daft's measure of innovation was calculated by a ranked assessment of innovations in a particular industry. More innovative firms adopt activities which were considered innovative by industry experts.

The findings of the Bantel and Jackson (1989) study demonstrated that educational and functional heterogeneity among top management team members positively influenced the number of innovations in banks. Bantel and Jackson (1989) concluded that educational and functional heterogeneity increases a team's cognitive resources and by extension raises the level of cognitive conflict within the team on strategic decisions. They also concluded that increasing these cognitive resources raises the number of innovative alternatives generated by the group and improves strategic decision making. This finding was tied directly to and extends Murray's (1989) study. Although Murray demonstrated that heterogeneity affected firm performance his study was unable to show why this relationship existed. In contrast, Bantel and Jackson's (1989) study gave insight into that process. Skill heterogeneity increased the cognitive abilities of the team and therefore the team makes better strategic decisions and improves organizational performance. Interestingly they did not find evidence of what they called "dysfunctional conflict" or what Amason (1996) labeled affective conflict. They noted that future studies should concentrate on the other effects of skill heterogeneity such as turnover and possible increases in dysfunctional conflict since they had not given these constructs sufficient attention.

Jackson et al.'s (1991) study extended the work of Bantel and Jackson (1989) by examining the role of functional and educational heterogeneity on top management team turnover and dysfunctional conflict. They measured team heterogeneity as the coefficient of variation between team member functional area, industry experience, educational level, and academic major in the highest degree just as Bantel and Jackson (1989) and Murray (1989) had earlier. They found that skill heterogeneity was a predictor of top management team turnover rates. A limitation of their study however was that they did not attempt to link these team behaviors to organizational performance. One could surmise that high turnover could hamper strategy implementation thereby harming firm performance. One can also surmise that this turnover stems from high levels of affective conflict. Based on these three studies, then, it can be postulated that skill heterogeneity, measured as educational or functional heterogeneity, increases the pool of cognitive resources available to a team (Bantel and Jackson, 1989), organizational performance in the long run, (Murray, 1989), and increases the level of affective or dysfunctional conflict and top management team turnover (Jackson et al., 1991), thereby potentially lowering firm performance in the short run as Murray (1989) suggested.

Harrison (1993) provided additional evidence about the link between skill heterogeneity and affective conflict. The objective of her study was to link individual differences, or heterogeneity, to group effectiveness. She linked individual differences to effectiveness through group cohesion which she argued was a most important team process. Harrison's sample, 788 work group employees from the plant of a *Fortune* 500 firm, included groups ranging in size from 5 to 15 members. Effectiveness was measured as a function of productivity, turnover intention, and the level of organizational commitment. Her data was collected using questionnaires, interviews, and existing plant data. Harrison's findings suggested that group heterogeneity on individual differences often has a negative effect on group cohesion and the effectiveness of work groups.

Even though Harrison studied lower level work teams, as opposed to top management teams, her work has interesting implications for the present research. She found a negative relationship between team heterogeneity with group cohesiveness and effectiveness. Hogg (1987) also found an inverse relationship with heterogeneity and group cohesion. Group cohesion was important to this project because it was a behavioral variable indicating the way that group members feel about each other. Group cohesion has been shown to have direct effects on the performance and effectiveness of groups (Bollen & Hoyle, 1990; Goodman et al., 1987). Cohesive groups were assumed to be more effective because highly cohesive groups can force members to comply to group norms (Festinger, 1950; Seashore, 1954). Group cohesion could be argued to have an inverse relationship with affective conflict (Kabanoff, 1991) and therefore could serve as a theoretical guide for this study in the development of hypotheses by linking skill heterogeneity to the level of affective conflict (Gladstein, 1984).

The tendency among most top management team researchers has been to consider top management team heterogeneity to have positive effects on firm performance (Pfeffer, 1983) while researchers studying work teams have found heterogeneity to harm performance. Two explanations can be offered for this discrepancy. First, the level of the group may make a difference. Heterogeneity may yield different results among top managers who operate in different contexts than other employees. This inconsistency could also stem from a failure to recognize that two types of conflict may exist among team members (Amason, 1996). If skill heterogeneity escalates cognitive conflict, then the effects on firm performance may ultimately be positive. But if skill heterogeneity raises affective conflict, there may be high team turnover and performance may fall. To date, the composition of top management teams has been shown to affect team turnover by creating a tense environment perhaps signifying affective conflict (Jackson et al., 1991; Wagner, Pfeffer, & O'Reilly, 1984; Wiersema & Bird, 1993). It has also been shown to increase organizational performance (Michel & Hambrick, 1992; Murray, 1989) and to facilitate strategic change by enhancing the commitment of a top management team to a particular strategic orientation (Wiersema & Bantel, 1992). These positive effects may stem from increased cognitive conflict.

What was clear was that the composition of the team has an effect on the actions or behaviors of the team. Jackson et al. (1991) found that team heterogeneity affected turnover and commitment in top management teams. Harrison (1993) found that group heterogeneity negatively affected turnover, organizational commitment, and group cohesion. Hogg (1987) had similar findings in his study. Murray (1989) found that skill heterogeneity has positive long term and negative short term effects on firm performance. Bantel and Jackson (1989) supported Murray's finding by expanding and clarifying the process by which skill heterogeneity improved firm performance through a top management team's cognitive resources. Jackson et al. (1991) found that team skill heterogeneity affected the propensity of team members to leave the firm. In other words, the way team members felt about the firm was associated with the differences between them and their cohorts.

## Skill Heterogeneity Evidence from Entrepreneurship Research

The scant evidence about skill heterogeneity from the entrepreneurship literature was mostly anecdotal. Kamm et al. (1990) offered some evidence as to the importance of teams in new venture performance. Along with Gartner (1985), they argued that skill-diverse teams handle the complexities of new ventures better than skill-homogeneous teams. In a rare empirical study of top management teams in new ventures, Roure and Maidique (1986) proposed two hypotheses which specifically relate to teams. The first hypothesis related to the possible link between what they called skill completeness and firm success. The second hypothesis related to the degree of prior joint business experience among entrepreneurial team members. Their study examined eight firms which were successfully funded by venture capitalists and which met three additional success criteria. First, each firm had been incorporated for at least three years. Second, each firm had reached sales of at least twenty million dollars. Third, each had achieved after tax profits greater than five percent of sales.

Roure and Maidique (1986) found that team skill completeness (which is, in essence, team skill heterogeneity) contributed directly to new venture success. Of the successful firms in their study, half were deemed to have high levels of skill heterogeneity. The degree of prior experience with entrepreneurial team members was also deemed an important characteristic of the successful new venture.

Siegel, Siegel, and Macmillian (1993) studied extremely high-growth new firms in an attempt to identify the characteristics of successful new ventures. Their sample was drawn from the Paul Reynolds' database of 1600 entrepreneurial firms in Pennsylvania. These firms were compiled through SBI and SBDC projects and had mean revenues of $1.35 million. All of the companies in this database had been started within five years of the administration of the questionnaire. Seigel et al., designed a questionnaire which gathered data on both strategic planning orientation and start-up team background information. They found that high-growth new ventures tend to be founded by teams. The important findings about teams from the Siegel et al. (1993) study relate to the functional balance of the team, a crude measure of skill heterogeneity. They argued that higher growth firms are better able to support fully developed management teams. At the same time, the statistical relationship can be interpreted two ways; it is not clear from their study if the fully developed team causes the firm to grow or if the growing firm creates enough resources to support the salaries of a fully developed entrepreneurial team.

Finally, Eisenhardt and Schoonhoven (1990) assessed the differences among top managers of entrepreneurial firms in an effort to understand why some firms grow to greatness and why others either die or remain small and become stagnant. They argued two things about organizational leaders in entrepreneurial firms. First, the leader(s) sometimes can and do influence the performance of entrepreneurial firms. Second, certain individuals or teams have the ability to influence new venture performance when others do not.

Eisenhardt and Schoonhoven's (1990) sample came from a master list of firms maintained by the Semiconductor Industry Association. All of the firms in the sample were high technology, semiconductor firms. Of a total sample size of 92, almost 70 percent were in Silicon Valley. Skill difference was operationalized as the differences among functional backgrounds and industry experience of team members. Eisenhardt and Schoonhoven found that entrepreneurial teams that have greater skill differences are better able to influence the performance of new ventures than are teams with more similar skills. This study's positive aspects include its focus on the team as a part of the assessment of the strategic actions of entrepreneurial firms.

## SUMMARY OF EVIDENCE ON THE SKILL HETEROGENEITY–CONFLICT LINK

Harrison (1993) found lower cohesion among heterogenous teams which as Kabanoff (1991) explains may indicate higher levels of affective conflict. Similarly, Jackson et al. (1991) found that heterogenous teams tend to have problems with turnover. Again, one could postulate that such teams may be experiencing affective conflict. Team members who simply don't like each other may be more apt to leave. Though these two studies lead to speculation about the presence of affective conflict, they do not provide any direct evidence that it exists. This research will look to see whether top management team skill heterogeneity increases the level of affective conflict. Hence the following hypothesis:

> *Hypothesis One A: Entrepreneurial team skill heterogeneity is positively related to the level of affective conflict.*

Several studies were presented above which offer evidence about skill heterogeneity and its link to the level of cognitive conflict. Two studies show how this process might work in top management teams. Bantel and Jackson (1989) explained their findings by arguing that skill heterogeneity increases a team's cognitive resources or abilities. These increased cognitive resources could explain why Murray found skill heterogeneity to have positive effects on firm performance. Taken together, these studies show a link between skill heterogeneity, the cognitive resources of top management, and firm performance. Others support this link. Roure and Madique's (1986) study of "skill completeness," for example, concurred with Murray's results. Kamm et al. (1990) and Kamm and Nurick (1993) argue that entrepreneurial team skill heterogeneity should improve strategic decisions and, therefore, new venture performance. Gartner (1985) argues that skill heterogeneity is important because of the complexity of new ventures.

Diversity of skills within an entrepreneurial team should increase the number of strategic perspectives offered by the entrepreneurial team (Virany and Tushman, 1986). If the number of perspectives or options is increased then by definition the level of cognitive conflict should increase (Schweiger, Sandberg, and Regan, 1986). Therefore the following hypothesis is offered:

> *Hypothesis One B: Entrepreneurial team skill heterogeneity is positively linked to the level of cognitive conflict.*

## EVIDENCE OF A LINK BETWEEN COGNITIVE AND AFFECTIVE CONFLICT, AND STRATEGIC ORIENTATION

As the discussion of the prior section indicates, two types of conflict may occur. In this section it will be argued that these two types may generate different consequences. Affective conflict, for instance, could be argued to impair the ability of the management team to agree on a particular strategic orientation because it affects the level of consensus existing among team members on the choice of a particular strategic orientation. Team members may not act for the good of the strategy because of their affectivity toward that strategy or toward other members who support the strategy. Affective conflict therefore may influence the level of commitment to a particular chosen strategy (Amason & Schweiger, 1994; Hambrick & Snow, 1977) and team members may act in a covert manner to undermine that strategic orientation (Kabanoff, 1991).

Cognitive conflict should directly affect the choice of strategic orientation because team members who disagree on key issues are more likely to evaluate additional viable strategic alternatives (Cosier & Schwenk, 1990; Schweiger, Sandberg, & Rechner, 1989). The importance of cognitive conflict within the executive team is supported by Schweiger et al.'s (1989) idea of devil's advocacy. The concept of devil's advocacy is simply that by increasing the levels of cognitive conflict between team members, the quality of strategic decisions improves.

Two studies of top management teams explore the value of raising cognitive conflict within the team to improve decision quality. The first of the these studies, by Schweiger, Sandberg and Regan (1986), concentrates on three main strategic decision making modes within top management teams. The first mode, dialectical inquiry, uses bates between diametrically opposed sets of recommendations. The second method, devil's advocacy, utilizes a critique of options under consideration at that time by the strategic group. The third method, a consensus oriented, decision-making model, helps the top management team reach agreement on the strategic decision. The objective of this research project was to determine which of these three techniques do more to improve strategic decision making.

Using thirty teams of M.B.A. students, with ten teams assigned to each decision-making method, the researchers explored each decision making mode and its decision effectiveness. Their findings show that the student teams with the most cognitive conflict made better strategic decisions. Dialectical inquiry and devil's advocacy both use cognitive conflict as their principal leverage point for improving strategic decisions. However, the use of students limits the generalizability of this study.

A similar study, by Schweiger et al. (1989), used managers as decision makers. The researchers hypothesized that dialectical inquiry and devil's advocacy will yield the best strategic decisions by rasing cognitive conflict and increasing the amount of discussion on a particular decision.

One hundred and twenty individuals, from three divisions of a *Fortune* 500 company, all participating in the company's executive development program, constitute the sample for this study. Of these, all were college graduates, 61 percent had master's degrees, and five percent held doctorates. Three judges, a vice-president, the director of strategic planning, and an educator in the field of strategic management rated the decision quality produced with each decision making method. The findings, that both dialectical inquiry and devil's advocacy yielded better decisions than the consensus approach to strategic decision making, confirmed the original hypothesis.

Amason (1996) tested the outcomes of both cognitive conflict and affective conflict in a study of strategic decision processes of top management teams among 48 food processing firms in the United States. He hypothesized that cognitive conflict improves the quality of strategic decisions but that decision quality decreases as the level of affective conflict rises within the top management team (Amason, 1996). As predicted, Amason found cognitive conflict to increase decision quality and affective conflict to decrease the commitment to strategic decisions. As an important aside Amason (1996) wrote that it was clear that some teams deal with affective conflict better than others.

The studies reviewed above give clear guidance on the link between the two types of conflict and strategic orientation. Cognitive conflict improves the strategic decisions which firms make (Amason, 1996). Affective conflict could affect the choice of strategic orientation and negatively influence organizational performance through the strategic implementation process (Amason, 1996; Kabanoff, 1991; Schwieger, Sandberg, and Regan, 1989; Cosier and Rose, 1977). The link between cognitive and affective conflict is also quite clear. Amason (1996) noted that only exceptional teams can raise the level of cognitive conflict and not raise the level affective conflict. In fact Amason found a direct relationship between the levels of cognitive and affective conflict. Affective conflict would rise as cognitive conflict rises because of the frustration associated with dealing with di-polar views of strategic orientation (Cosier and Rose, 1977). Kabanoff (1991) argues that affective conflict can incite team members to act covertly to destroy commitment to a particular strategic orientation if a team member feels that their ideas are being unfairly dismissed.

Two of Eisenhardt's studies are relevant to this discussion because they utilize entrepreneurial samples and measure top management team variables. Eisenhart's (1989) study examined those factors which are linked to the speed of strategic decisions. Two research questions were posed: First, how fast are strategic decisions made? Second, does decision speed affect the performance of the firm? Several team level variables were measured, including team size, the number of strategic alternatives considered by the team at any one time, and the need for consensus among team members. Eisenhardt used a sample of eight microcomputer firms, which ranged in size from 50 to 500 employees. Using a multiple interview method, two different interviewers met with at least five subjects from each firm on consecutive days. Questionnaires containing the same questions asked in these interviews were administered to the top management group.

Eisenhardt's (1989) findings are valuable to the present study for several reasons. In showing that entrepreneurial teams which consider larger numbers of alternatives make faster and "better" decisions, an additional piece of evidence is gained concerning the link between cognitive conflict and strategic orientation. The larger number of strategic alternatives creates a greater opportunity for cognitive conflict. This ties directly to the two studies by Schweiger et al., (1986; 1989) which found that larger numbers of alternatives yield higher levels of cognitive conflict and better strategic decisions. Though this research did not explicitly examine affective conflict, Eisenhardt (1989) found that entrepreneurial firms in her study either worked diligently to resolve interpersonal conflict between team members or ignored it all together. If the conflict over a particular decision was too great and consensus was not obtained, then the CEO and the functionally relevant entrepreneurial team member made the decision. This "round robin" effect, a situation in which leadership of the team was handed from team member to team member depending on the decision to be made, is often expected in entrepreneurial firms because of the survivability factors related to firm newness.

In a study using a similar methodology, Eisenhardt and Bourgeois (1988) attempted to find the role of political behavior and personal conflict in entrepreneurial teams. They used a sample of eight microcomputer firms, which ranged in size from 50 to 500 employees. Using a multiple interview method, two different interviewers met with at least five subjects from each firm on consecutive days. Questionnaires containing the same questions asked in these interviews were administered to the top management group. They found that conflict within the team progresses into either a political problem (affective conflict) or into an open discussion (cognitive conflict) about the many strategic alternatives which might exist. Although affective conflict was often present in these entrepreneurial firms, it had a secondary effect. They argue that affective conflict is detrimental to the firm only when the power of the CEO is high and political coalitions are developed to push a particular viewpoint. Since political coalitions are less often developed in entrepreneurial firms because of firm size (Mintzberg, 1983), it would be difficult for affective conflict to have its expected effects. Entrepreneurial team members attempt to deal with their personality conflicts with other team members so that the speed and quality of decisions will not be affected (Eisenhardt and Bourgeois, 1988). Since entrepreneurial firms are so often under threat, the existence of the firm is more important to the entrepreneur than conflicts with other entrepreneurial team members. Thus it is likely that the firm may perform as if affective conflict does not exist.

Another work which deals with the concept of conflict and consensus in the entrepreneurial team is by West and Meyer (1994). The main objective of their study was to show that consensus oriented decision making in entrepreneurial firms has negative performance implications. That is, consensus by the entrepreneurial team on strategic decisions leads to poor organizational performance. They argue that entrepreneurship exists in a "world of ideas" and that consensus on strategic decisions reduces the number of feasibly considered alternatives. West and Meyer argue that multiple ideas should be encouraged and therefore imply that the level of entrepreneurial team cognitive conflict should be increased as much as possible. Their sample was 51 Colorado companies from computer, software, and microelectronics industries. Nearly all of the firms were private corporations and would be classified as entrepreneurial firms because of their growth rate, size, and strategic orientation. The average number of employees in each firm was 60 and most of the respondents characterized their main strategic objective as firm-wide asset and sales growth. West and Meyer measured consensus by a method which calculates the sum of the squared distances between the CEO's ideas about business level strategy and the entrepreneurial team member's ideas of business level strategy.

The findings of this study are valuable and relevant to this research because of their interesting conclusions about consensus on business level strategy and the number of strategic options considered during their strategic planning cycle. West and Meyer (1994) found that consensus among entrepreneurial team members on the means to achieve the goals has a negative impact on firm performance. They concluded that the reason that consensus on strategy has a negative effect on performance is that once consensus had been gained, the number of real strategic alternatives considered in the future is reduced. The reduction in the number of strategic alternatives considered should reduce the amount of cognitive conflict within the entrepreneurial team about strategic decisions.

Schweiger et al., (1986; 1989) would argue that cognitive conflict could be linked to the quality of the decisions in West and Meyer's (1994) study. Eisenhart's (1989) work is also applicable here since she found that better decisions are made by considering larger numbers of alternatives. All of these studies found a link between the number of alternatives considered and the quality of the decisions made or the performance of the firm. Schweiger et al. (1986; 1989) linked cognitive conflict to the quality of decisions. West and Meyer (1994) omitted the decision step in the process and attempted to link the number of alternatives considered, a possible surrogate for cognitive conflict, to firm performance. Eisenhart (1989) did much the same thing. Taken together these studies show a two step process. Cognitive conflict arises from considering multiple alternatives. Cognitive conflict improves the strategic decisions firms make and therefore improves firm performance.

Virany and Tushman (1986) studied the role of entrepreneurial team replacements on firm performance. Their research explored the skills and characteristics of new team members and their effect on the firm's ability to adapt and perform well financially. They hypothesized that replacement team members give entrepreneurial firms the ability to adapt more readily to changes in the environment because of the new strategic perspectives bring to the firm (the addition of the new perspective implies an increase in the level of cognitive conflict within the firm).

Virany and Tushman (1986) studied 59 minicomputer firms from the time of their establishment, between 1968 and 1971 until 1980, their demise, or their acquisition. Their data, gathered from 10-Ks, annual reports, industry journals and business press, and interviews with industry experts, included information on executive team characteristics, succession events, organizational performance, industry background, functional background, team tenure, firm tenure, presence of the founder in the team, and ownership. Twenty-five of the firms were viable when their longitudinal study was complete.

Virany and Tushman (1986) found that if team members who were leaving were replaced with team members holding a very different set of skills, the firm was able to adapt to changes and perform better. They assumed that background, whether it be experience or functional, was a surrogate for the skills of the team member. This may not be the case. Still this work provides further evidence about the nature and importance of the skill composition of entrepreneurial teams. The inclusion of a new member of the entrepreneurial team should change the level of cognitive conflict among team members by raising the number of strategic perspectives within the group. Whether this change occurs via the set of skills of the new team member or is simply based on the new member's differing strategic perspective is not clear, but the new team member changes the level of skill heterogeneity and possibly cognitive conflict within the team. Virany and Tushman argue that this change improves organizational decision making and performance.

## SUMMARY OF EVIDENCE ON CONFLICT

The evidence shown here supports the idea that cognitive conflict positively affects the choice of strategic orientation in new ventures. Eisenhardt (1989) found that the consideration of multiple alternatives had positive effects on new venture performance. West and Meyer (1994) found the number of strategic alternatives considered by the team should be as high as possible. Virany and Tushman (1986) found that different views or perspectives improved the decision making abilities of new venture teams. David Schweiger's group (1986, 1989) found in their studies of top management teams that cognitive conflict had a positive effect on firm performance. Amason (1996; 1993) found that cognitive conflict improved the decisions made by top management teams. The evidence is consistent and strong: cognitive conflict has a positive effect on strategic decision making.

Amason (1996) argues that almost without exception it is difficult to alter the level of cognitive conflict without increasing the level of affective conflict. He argues, in fact, that the main issue in managing conflict is related to the idea of keeping control of affective conflict in the midst of rising cognitive conflict. Therefore Hypothesis 2 "A" is offered:

> *Hypothesis Two A: Among entrepreneurial team members, the level of cognitive conflict is linked positively with the level of affective conflict.*

Eisenhardt (1989) provides an indication that the higher the level of cognitive conflict in an entrepreneurial team, the faster and better the decisions. The increase in decision quality leads Eisenhardt to this conclusion: considering several opposing options improves the performance of the firm. Amason and Schweiger (1994) and Schweiger et al. (1986, 1989) lend support to the notion that cognitive conflict levels within the entrepreneurial team are associated with "better" choice of strategic orientation and new venture performance.

Studies by Eisenhardt (1989), Virany and Tushman (1986), and West and Meyer (1994) support the notion that improved strategic choices result from higher levels of cognitive conflict. Studies by David Schweiger and his colleagues (1986, 1989) on established firm top management teams show clearly that higher levels of cognitive conflict improve the quality of strategic decisions. Amason (1996) also found support for this idea.

The question then is what is an improved strategic choice in an entrepreneurial firm? Miller (1983) describes an entrepreneurial strategic orientation as risky, proactive, and innovative. Miller and Friesen (1983) describe the successful entrepreneurial strategy as future oriented. Miller and Friesen (1982) described the entrepreneurial strategic orientation as analytical. Miller and Camp (1985) found that successful new venture strategies tended to be of an aggressive nature. Covin (1991) and Covin and Slevin (1989) argue that new ventures should focus on strategic orientations with these characteristics for new venture success. If cognitive conflict yields "better" strategic decisions then entrepreneurial team members should choose entrepreneurial strategic orientations to improve new venture performance. These literature streams are the foundation for the second hypothesis which relates directly to the link between cognitive conflict, and an entrepreneurial strategic orientation. Thus Hypothesis Two "B"is:

*Hypothesis Two B: Cognitive conflict among entrepreneurial team members is positively linked to an entrepreneurial strategic orientation.*

Given the proposed link between cognitive conflict and affective conflict in Hypothesis Two "A" it would be theoretically incomplete to exclude affective conflict from discussions of strategic choice. Two perspectives seem to exist on this subject. Amason (1996) and Kabanoff (1991) both provide support for a link between affective conflict and strategic choice. Amason (1996) and Jehn (1992) find that affective conflict is a powerful force in decisions made by groups of managers. They argue that affective conflict can have detrimental effects on strategic decision making. Eisenhardt and Bourgeois (1988) argue that top management teams are capable of ignoring social conflict and focusing on the decisions to be made. They argued that this type of conflict did little to alter the commitment of top management team members. Since the direction of the relationship is unclear in new ventures the hypothesis is posed without a sign. Thus Hypothesis Two "C" is:

*Hypothesis Two C: Affective conflict is linked to strategic orientation.*

## EVIDENCE OF DIRECT EFFECTS OF AFFECTIVE CONFLICT ON NEW VENTURE PERFORMANCE

Kabanoff (1991) argues that affective conflict can pervade an organization and have debilitating effects on firm performance. Eisenhardt and Bourgeois (1988) find that affective conflict might exist in entrepreneurial firms, but that it is often ignored because team members recognize the need for organizational survival. Thus Hypothesis Two "D":

*Hypothesis Two D: Affective conflict will have a negative relationship to new venture performance.*

## THE BUSINESS STRATEGY AND FIRM PERFORMANCE LINK

The link between strategy and organizational performance has been a common theme in strategic management research for several years (Andrews, 1971; Child, 1972; Rumelt, 1986; Porter, 1980; Dess & Davis, 1984). In a recent meta-analysis Capon, Farley and Hoenig (1990) found a link between performance and strategy in most of the 320 articles used in their study. In entrepreneurial firms this link is also well established. Appendix C contains a sample of studies which have attempted empirically to link business strategy and organizational performance. Most of the research in Appendix C studied entrepreneurial firms. These studies attempted to link entrepreneurial strategic postures to new venture performance.

### What Is an Entrepreneurial Strategic Posture?

The firms in this study are entrepreneurial firms. Covin (1991) and Covin and Slevin (1989) argue that entrepreneurial firms grow faster and achieve higher levels of market share with more entrepreneurial strategic postures. Miller (1983) and Miller and Friesen (1982) described the entrepreneurial strategic posture as "risk-taking, innovative, future oriented (futurity), analytic, and proactive (Miller, 1983 p.777)." The conservative strategic posture would simply be the opposite of the entrepreneurial strategic orientation. Venkatraman (1989) added theoretical work from others, and added two additional dimensions called defensiveness and aggressiveness to this list. Miller and Camp (1985) found that successful entrepreneurial firms tended to adopt strategies which could be characterized as aggressive. The importance of Venkatraman's study and scale development effort is that he tested the reliability and validity of the strategic orientation dimensions and then attempted to link the dimensions with firm performance.

## Theoretical Foundations for the Strategy-Performance Link in New Ventures

Several empirical tests of the strategy dimensions and their link to performance have been conducted. Sandberg (1986) found that strategy is an important predictor of new venture performance. In an extension of Sandberg's work, McDougall et al. (1992) found that strategy and the interaction of strategy and industry were important predictors of new venture performance. Their sample included 247 small high technology firms. They identified several strategy types instead of measuring strategy as a dimension. McDougall et al. (1992) attempted to identify specific strategies that were successful in new ventures instead of identifying the characteristics of successful strategies. They concluded that some of the strategies McDougall (1987) identified worked well some of the time and others worked well at other times depending on the structure of the industry. McDougall et al. (1992) made a strong empirical case for an interaction effect between new venture strategy and industry structure.

Covin (1991) and Covin and Slevin (1989) found a connection between performance and strategic orientation. In both cases, their samples included about 160 small manufacturing firms in Georgia. Covin and Slevin (1989) concluded that the link between strategic orientation and new venture performance existed but varied according to whether the firm operated in a hostile or benign environment. Firms that adopted entrepreneurial strategic postures performed well in hostile environments. Firms that adopted conservative strategic postures performed well in benign environments. Covin (1991) concluded that firms that were at the ends of the strategy dimensions out-performed their counterparts toward the center. In other words, conservative firms performed as well as the entrepreneurial firms as long as they committed themselves to that particular strategic orientation. The firms at the ends of the strategic dimensions performed well and those firms that waffled between the two strategic orientations exhibited lower financial performance.

Venkatraman's (1989) studied two hundred and twelve firms from the *Directory of Corporate Affiliations* in a study which improved the scales used to measure the dimensions of business level strategy and attempted to link the dimensions of strategic posture to firm performance. The outcome of his study was important because it ties the strategy dimensions to the performance of the firm through a latent construct model. The problem with the study was the use of perceptual measures of firm performance.

Tan and Lichert (1994) also used a dimensionality approach to the measurement of strategy. They attempted to find the link between environment, strategy, and performance. One hundred eighty firms were randomly selected from groups of firms in three industrial cities in North China. They found, in a regulated economy, that a defensive strategic posture, or what Miller and Friesen (1982) would call a conservative strategic posture seemed to be positively linked with performance.

Zahra and Covin (1993) also tested the link between strategy and performance using a methodology similar to Venkatraman (1989) but they note that their strategic orientation dimensions lack the "conceptual completeness of the STROBE scale (p. 456.)" One hundred and three manufacturing firms in hostile environments were chosen from twenty-eight SIC codes. The strategic orientation dimensions of riskiness, innovativeness, and proactivness were directly linked to firm performance. Zahra and Covin also found a contingency relationship between strategy and technology policy that had an effect on performance. Simply, a fit between strategy and technology policy increased firm performance.

These studies show that when strategy was conceived and measured as a dimension, it can be linked to firm performance. There was support here to argue that conservative firms that fully adopt the conservative strategic posture would outperform firms stuck between the conservative and entrepreneurial strategic postures. Fully committed entrepreneurial firms should also outperform muddlers.

## SUMMARY OF FINDINGS ON THE LINK BETWEEN STRATEGIC ORIENTATION AND PERFORMANCE

Consistent evidence has been presented which shows a positive relationship between strategic orientation and new venture performance. New ventures that commit and pursue entrepreneurial strategic orientations should outperform those that do not take such actions (Covin and Slevin, 1989; Covin, 1991). A link between the choice of strategic orientation and new venture performance is consistent and clear and found in many studies (Chandler and Hanks, 1994; Covin, 1991; Covin and Slevin, 1989; McDougall et al., 1992; Miller and Friesen, 1982; Naman and Slevin, 1993; Sandberg, 1986; Sterns et al., 1995).

Most of the literature in strategic management on strategy and performance attempts to provide an empirical link between strategy and performance (Covin, 1991; Covin & Slevin, 1989; Miller, 1983; Miller & Friesen, 1982). In new venture research, business level strategy was shown to explain a great deal of the variation in new venture performance (McDougall et al., 1992). Sandberg's (1986) new venture performance model linked strategic orientation with performance. Recently Lumpkin and Dess (1996) recently posited that successful new ventures adopt strategies which have certain characteristics. Miller (1983) described the entrepreneurial strategic orientation as one that is future oriented, risky, innovative, and proactive. Miller and Camp (1985) tied aggressive new venture strategies to new venture performance. Miller and Friesen (1982) and Covin (1991) found that entrepreneurial strategic orientations which were characteristically analytical improved new venture performance. Covin (1991) and Covin and Slevin (1989) argued that a new venture that adopts and focuses on a strategic orientation which was characteristically proactive, analytical, risky, aggressive, and future oriented was prone to improve new venture performance. Thus the third set of hypotheses is:

*Hypothesis Three A: Proactive strategic orientations will be positively linked to new venture performance.*

*Hypothesis Three B: Analytical strategic orientations will be positively linked to new venture performance.*

*Hypothesis Three C: Risky strategic orientations will be positively linked to new venture performance.*

*Hypothesis Three D: Aggressive strategic orientations will be positively linked to new venture performance.*

*Hypothesis Three E: Future oriented strategic orientations will be positively linked to new venture performance.*

The link between strategic orientation and firm performance was certainly supported by the above empirical evidence but the environment has been shown to have an effect on the strength of that relationship (Prescott, 1986). The next sub-section reviews the literature on industry effects and its relationship to strategy and new venture performance.

## THE EXTENSION OF THE NEW VENTURE PERFORMANCE MODEL TO INCLUDE ENVIRONMENT

This section includes a discussion on why the new venture performance model will be redesigned to include a full conception of the environment rather than simply industry structure. Sandberg (1986) was among the first to attempt to control for the effects various environments might have on strategy and performance of new ventures. Sandberg (1986) studied seventeen new ventures in Atlanta, Houston, and New York. Ventures were selected based on their choice as fundable by a venture capital firm. He argued that industry structure and industry life cycle stage were important factors in new venture performance. McDougall et al., (1992) found that the interaction of strategy and industry, measured as industry barriers and industry concentration, was an important variable in the new venture performance model. In a recent article Stearns, Carter, Reynolds and Williams (1995) support McDougall's findings. They measured the industry as nine broad industry categories.

Dess, Ireland and Hitt (1990) reviewed fifty articles that attempted to control for environmental or industry effects. Only eleven of the studies appeared to have any credibility because of the methodological inadequacies of the other studies reviewed. These inadequacies included lack of data, use of researcher judgement to place a firm in a particular industry category, and overall lack of conceptualization of environmental dimensions. These eleven studies showed that, without controlling for the environment, the findings of the research were suspect and that by controlling for the environment, researchers captured knowledge about strategies and their relationship to the environment which had not existed before. Some of the studies chose single industry samples, which controls for industry effects, but these studies have limited value because of their lack of generalizability across industries. Other studies used some single dimension to measure the environment such as industry concentration or SIC code. Dess et al. (1990) argue that such conceptualizations of the environment are "inadequate assessments of reality." Few of the studies did a sufficient job conceptualizing the environment. Similarly, few of the studies which included industry or environmental information within the field of entrepreneurship have done a sufficient job conceptualizing the environment (Sandberg, 1986; McDougall et al., 1992).

Based on this evaluation, the contributions of Sandberg and McDougall can still be viewed as important to the field of entrepreneurship, but it is clear that their conceptualization of the environment is incomplete. Dess and Beard (1984), classify environments by industry concentration, environmental complexity, and instability. The inclusion of these three environmental dimensions is justified by the research summarized in Appendix C. This table shows clearly that the three environmental dimensions called complexity, munificence, and dynamism have received consistent empirical support. By incorporating this more comprehensive view of the environment the new venture performance model would be extended as follows:

$$NVP = f(ET, S, Env, S \times Env)$$

Where NVP is equal to the new venture performance model, S is equal to strategy, Env is equal to the environment, and S x Env is equal to the interaction of strategy and environment.

The next section reviews specific literature on the findings about the environmental dimensions and their interactions with strategic orientation and the interaction's proposed effect on performance. Evidence is presented which supports the idea of a positive interaction between an entrepreneurial strategic orientation and new venture performance.

## EVIDENCE OF THE RELATIONSHIPS BETWEEN ENVIRONMENT-STRATEGY-PERFORMANCE

Previous studies found a relationship between strategy and environment. Prescott (1986) found that the environment moderates the strength of the relationship between strategy and performance. Prescott's used industrial organizational economics as a theoretical base. The main measure of the environment in his study is industry structure. He used dummy variables to assign each of the firms in his study to one of Porter's (1980) eight generic industry structures. Prescott's sample included 1638 business units in the PIMS database. His work is important because it shows that environment moderates the strength of the relationship but not the particular aspects of strategy that affect performance. He suggested that future research should concentrate on industry sub-classes rather than major industry groups because of aggregation problems he had at the three digit SIC code level.

In a sample of one hundred small firms, Nwachukwu and Tsalikis (1989) found that the heterogeneity of an environment was a defining factor in firm performance. They defined a heterogenous environment as one in which many industry players pursue very different strategies. They used four questionnaire items to assess environmental heterogeneity. Their measure of firm performance was return on investment. This study used two questionnaire items to measure strategy and four questionnaire items to measure the external environment. They found that entrepreneurial strategies that are risky and proactive interact with a complex and dynamic environment positively to affect performance.

Miller and Friesen's (1983) study on the link between strategy and environment attempts to understand the relationship between certain strategic orientations and the elements of external environment. Miller and Friesen operationalized the environment as comprised of three dimensions including: dynamism (or rate and degree of change), hostility, and environmental heterogeneity which is closely related to industry concentration. Strategy was conceptualized as a dimension with end points of entrepreneurial and conservative strategic orientations (Miller and Friesen, 1982).

Miller and Friesen (1983) found that successful firms in dynamic, hostile, and heterogenous environments tended to adopt strategies which could be characterized as future oriented, analytic, risky, innovative, and proactive. They found a direct link between strategic orientation, type of environment, and firm success.

In a replication of the Dess and Beard (1984) study, McArthur and Nystrom (1991) found that the three environmental dimensions, dynamism, complexity, and munificence, all had an effect on the relationship between strategy and performance. Their sample included 109 large firms in thirty-five manufacturing industries. Although their findings supported the proposition that strategy and environment interact to affect firm performance, their study had one major problem. Their environmental data was from the late sixties and early seventies and might have little relation to today's environment. They measured strategy over ten years later.

In another study that utilized the original Dess and Beard (1984) measures of the environment, Keats and Hitt (1988) found the external environment to be the strongest force on their sample of firms. In a regression model the environmental measures explained a larger amount of the variation in organizational performance than any other variable including strategy. They used proxies for some of the variables in Dess and Beard's original data set but they used a three by three multi-trait, multi-method matrix to solve the measurement problems with their proxies. This study is somewhat unique because the researchers focused on the corporate level strategy as opposed to business level strategy. They found that all of the environmental dimensions had some effect on firm performance and corporate strategy. Dynamism however, explained the largest amount of variance in the organizational variables. Their project is important because it is the first study of this type to go beyond manufacturing firms as the study sample.

McDougall et al.'s, (1992) contribution to the new venture performance model is one of understanding the concept of "fit" in new venture performance. McDougall et al. found that industry concentration, measured as entry barriers and four digit SIC code, explains a significant portion of new venture performance. Based on a sample of 247 new ventures from the computer and communications industry, McDougall found that the interaction between industry and strategy explained a great deal of the variance in new venture performance. The problems with McDougall's work related to the environment are two-fold. First, her conception of the environment as simply industry concentration and industry barriers was incomplete. Second, her sample came from only two industries which greatly limits the generalizability of her study.

Covin and Slevin (1989) conducted a study on small firms in two types of environments. The objective of their study was to categorize attempts by smaller firms to create "effective strategic responses" to a hostile environment. Their sample consisted of 161 small manufacturers in Georgia. They measured environmental hostility on a three item scale suggested by Khandwalla (1976, 1977). They measured strategic orientation as Miller and Friesen did in 1982. This study is important because they found a link between environmental hostility (similar to Sharfman and Dean's (1991) competitive threat dimension) and an entrepreneurial strategic orientation. Firms that are more proactive and future oriented survive hostile environments better than firms that act like Miles and Snow's defenders.

Naman and Slevin (1993) argue that "fit" between environment and strategy is an important factor in new venture performance. They proposed that an entrepreneurial strategic orientation interacts with dynamic and hostile environments to influence performance positively. Their sample included 82 manufacturing firms in Southwestern Pennsylvania. They measured environmental dynamism and hostility with eight questionnaire items on a seven point scale (Miller and Friesen, 1982; Khandwalla, 1977). Strategy was measured with Miller and Friesen's (1982) strategic orientation scale. They found that firms whose strategies are proactive, risky, and innovative succeed in turbulent environments. Specifically, they found interaction effects among the three dimensions measuring strategy and the two dimensions used in their study to measure the environment. This study is important because it gives specific empirical findings on the interaction of strategic orientation and environmental dimensions.

In a recent study, Stearns et al. (1995) found additional evidence of an interaction effect between industry, strategy, and new venture performance. Their sample included 1900 new ventures. They proposed that the new venture's physical location had a significant influence on firm performance but they were only able to support the interaction effect found previously by McDougall et al. (1992). This article is important because it gives large sample support to the role of the environment in the new venture performance model.

## SUMMARY OF EVIDENCE ON THE LINK BETWEEN STRATEGY-ENVIRONMENT-PERFORMANCE

Two conclusions can be drawn from studies that utilize environment as one of the major variables in their models. First, the environment has some effect on the strategy-performance link of most businesses. Second, past research has tended to "oversimplify reality" and failed to conceptualize the environment fully (Keats and Hitt, 1988). New venture research has a contribution to add to these discoveries. Interaction effects tend to exist between new venture strategies, environment, and affect new venture performance.

Therefore the environment was approached in the following way in this study. First, it was assumed that new venture performance would be affected by the environment and therefore, this construct is an integral part of the new venture performance model. Second, the utilization of industry structure variables to measure the whole of the environment was incomplete and a more complete conceptualization of the environment was necessary to test the relationships between new venture performance, and the strategic orientation-environment interaction. Third, given the past findings in new venture research, it was assumed that strategic orientation and environment interacted to affect performance.

Many authors have proposed linkages between environmental dimensions and organizational variables (Andrews, 1971; Blau & Schoenherr, 1971; Burns & Stalker, 1961; Grinyer & Yasai-Ardekani, 1981; Hofer & Schendel, 1978; Lawrence & Lorsch, 1969; Pfeffer and Salanick, 1978; Thompson, 1967). It was the objective of the environments section of this chapter to create a theoretical frame for the role of the environment in new ventures. These studies and empirical studies specific to new ventures such as Sandberg (1986) and McDougall (1992) found that environment had a direct affect on new venture performance. Thus the fourth set of hypotheses:

> *Hypothesis Four A: Complexity will be linked to new venture performance.*
>
> *Hypothesis Four B: Dynamism will be linked to new venture performance.*
>
> *Hypothesis Four C: Competitive threat will be linked to new venture performance.*

It appears that the most appropriate view of the role of the environment in the new venture performance model would be as an interaction variable with strategic orientation. The interaction variable would therefore have a positive influence on new venture performance (McDougall et al., 1992; Naman and Slevin, 1993; Stearns et al., 1995).

Naman and Slevin (1993), for instance, found that the environmental dimensions of dynamism and hostility interact positively with an entrepreneurial strategic orientation and affect performance. Miller and Friesen (1983) found that riskiness, futurity, proactiveness, and analysis, four of the five strategy dimensions in the strategy scale used in this study, interacted positively with environments characterized as complex, dynamic, and hostile. Covin and Slevin (1989) found that munificence or competitive threat positively interacted with an entrepreneurial strategic orientation to affect performance. Some general connection seems to exist between high levels of environmental change, complexity, and competitive threat and an entrepreneurial strategic orientation. Thus the fifth set of hypotheses:

> *Hypothesis Five A: The interaction of Dynamism with an entrepreneurial strategic orientation will positively link to new venture performance.*
>
> *Hypothesis Five B: The interaction of Complexity with an entrepreneurial strategic orientation will positively link to new venture performance.*
>
> *Hypothesis Five C: The interaction of Competitive Threat with an entrepreneurial strategic orientation will positively link to new venture performance.*

The proceeding hypotheses are meant to capture all of the interactions between the different dimensions of strategy and environment. It seems likely that all of the relationships between the interactions of the three environmental variables and the five strategy variables and new venture performance will be positive.

The purpose of this literature review was to create a theoretical framework for the model presented in Chapter One. Four streams of literature were reviewed, five major hypotheses were developed, and the groundwork for the rest of the dissertation was laid. The next chapter deals with research design, and methodological considerations.

# CHAPTER 3

# Research Methodology

The objective of this chapter is to discuss the research methodology utilized in this study. The chapter includes the interview process, the questionnaire to be used, and the statistical techniques to be employed. This chapter is arranged in the following manner. The first section defines the terms specific to this research project. The second section describes the sample utilized in this study. The third section contains a discussion of the sequence of steps by which data collection will be completed. This section will also discuss the reliability and validity estimates of the measures used in this project. The final section of this chapter will discuss the statistical methods employed in this research and will explain how each specific hypothesis will be tested.

Campbell & Fiske (1959) emphasize that the use of multiple methodologies and sources of data ensures greater accuracy in the measurement of a phenomenon. Denzin (1978) argues that no single method can be used to explain a phenomenon because each method reveals different aspects of empirical reality. Different sources of data exist for many of the dimensions in the model in Appendix B.

## DEFINITIONS OF TERMS SPECIFIC TO THIS STUDY

In this study several terms are used in ways which are not common in other studies. The first and most important of these terms is the entrepreneurial team. Kamm et al. (1990) define an entrepreneurial team as "two or more individuals who jointly establish a firm in which they have a financial interest" (p. 7). Ensley and Banks (1992) and Gartner et al.

(1994) extend this definition to include those individuals who have direct strategic influence. For the purposes of this study, an individual who meets two of these three criteria will be considered part of the entrepreneurial team. Specifically, the three criteria include membership on the founding executive team, financial interest in the firm in excess of ten percent, and direct influence on strategic decisions.

Entrepreneurial team skill heterogeneity is defined in this study as the range of skills which team members possess. Simply, if one team member has leadership skills and one team member has administrative skills, then the team is considered to have higher skill heterogeneity than an entrepreneurial team with two members who are high on leadership skills. This definition differs from that used by Murray (1989) and Bantel and Jackson (1989) who equated skill heterogeneity with difference in functional areas among team members. Because individuals from different department may or may not have different skills, it is important to consider the skills themselves. Hambrick (1993) argues that use of measures other than demographic variables could offer new insights into existing phenomena.

The two types of conflict investigated in this study are cognitive and affective conflict. Cognitive conflict is the type of conflict which an entrepreneurial team experiences when its members are considering several alternative solutions to a particular strategic problem (Cosier & Rose, 1977). Cognitive conflict is likely to emerge in an entrepreneurial team because of the differing perspectives on strategic issues, various strategic decisions, and, ultimately, on the overall strategic direction of the firm (Amason & Schweiger, 1994). Cognitive conflict is the conflict of different ideas. It is task oriented; that is, it is directed toward the task(s) which the entrepreneurial team faces.

Affective conflict is directed toward entrepreneurial team members (Amason & Schweiger, 1994; Cosier & Rose, 1977; Edwards & Scullion, 1982; Jehn, 1992). It erupts in the form of personality conflicts among members of the entrepreneurial team. Because affective conflict involves the kind of disagreements that occur between people, it often occurs when conversations about ideas become personal criticisms of those who have forwarded differing opinions about a particular problem facing the firm. Edwards and Scullion (1982) argued that this type of non-directed conflict has debilitating effects on the abilities of members of executive teams to be productive.

The next construct examined in this research is business level strategy. For the purposes of this study, the terms *business level strategy, strategic posture*, and *strategic orientation* are used interchangeably. For a new venture, the choice of strategy basically evolves to a choice between a conservative strategic orientation and an entrepreneurial strategic orientation. Prior research has used a "dimensionality approach" to measure strategic orientation on a continuum between entrepreneurial and conservative endpoints (Covin, 1991; Covin & Slevin, 1989; Miller, 1983; Miller & Friesen, 1982; Naman and Slevin, 1993).

Entrepreneurial strategies would be more risky, proactive, analytical, aggressive, and future oriented. From this perspective any decision that increases the thrust of entrepreneurial activity or enhances the full adoption of an entrepreneurial strategic orientation should improve the performance of that particular firm (Covin and Slevin, 1989; Covin, 1991; Miller, 1983). The next section defines each of the dimensions comprising an entrepreneurial strategy.

Riskiness (Miller and Friesen, 1982; Venkatraman, 1989) is defined as the level of risk taken with firm resources. The riskiness dimension is not intended as a measure of entrepreneurial team risk propensity. The risk characteristics of actions or decisions made by entrepreneurial team members are what is important here. "What is the level of risk to firm resources regarding this firm's current strategic orientation" is the main question associated with this construct. Entrepreneurial firms typically place firm resources at greater risk than other firms (Miller, 1983; Covin, 1991).

Aggressiveness is defined as the posture adopted by firms attempting to improve market position. A more aggressive firm would allocate resources in such a way that they could improve market position faster than other firms in the same market. Vesper (1990) and Venkatraman (1989) noted that this type of behavior is related to the level of product innovation and market development. Entrepreneurial firms would tend to be market aggressors (Covin, 1991; Miller and Friesen, 1982; Miller and Camp, 1985).

Analysis is defined as the overall problem-solving posture of the new venture. Miller and Friesen (1984) refer to this characteristic as the tendency to search deeper to solve problems and generate the largest number of alternative solutions. Miller and Friesen (1983 and 1984) found that analysis was correlated with an entrepreneurial strategic orientation.

Futurity (Covin, 1991; Miller and Friesen, 1982; Venkatraman, 1989) is the idea of a desired future. Specifically, futurity is related to the choice between efficiency and effectiveness. This dimension is concerned with whether one wishes to take a long-term or short-term orientation. New ventures have been found to take a long-term view (Miller and Friesen, 1983).

Proactiveness (Covin, 1991; Miller and Friesen, 1982) refers to the tendency to take actions before they are necessary. This dimension is concerned with the search for market opportunities and experimentation in response to environmental needs. New ventures with entrepreneurial strategic orientations would tend to be quite proactive (Miller and Friesen, 1983; Miller, 1983). The combination of these dimensions gives a profile of the overall strategic orientation of the firm.

One should note that two approaches exist concerning the conceptualization of strategy in models which include team behavioral variables such as conflict and organizational variables such as strategy. Recently Amason (1996) used the single strategic decision methodology. This methodology has some advantages. Less noise or error should occur in models conceived with single decision methodologies. The level of conflict in these types of studies is related to a specific decision instead of all of business level strategy.

The use of overall strategic orientation also has some advantages. By studying firm strategic orientation, the researcher gains a much better understanding of the overall effects of conflict. By using strategic orientation rather than a single strategic decision, this project will not be subject to range restriction problems which are possible in single decision methodologies. By way of example, affective conflict may be high on one decision and low on another depending on the involvement of individual team members. The use of strategic orientation rather than a single strategic decision does not subject the findings of the research to the aberrations of one decision.

Environment is another important construct in this research. Here, it is defined and measured as a firm's task environment. Three environmental dimensions are utilized to describe a firm's task environment. These dimensions are dynamism, complexity, and environmental munificence or competitive threat. The next three paragraphs discuss the variables which are a part of the conceptual makeup of these three environmental dimensions.

Dynamism (Duncan, 1972; Lawrence and Lorsch, 1969; Dess and Beard, 1984; Sharfman and Dean, 1991) is defined as the way in which the elements of a task environment change. Less dynamism would mean that an industry is quite stable. Higher dynamism would mean that an environment lacks stability.

Complexity (Child, 1972; Duncan, 1972; Dess and Beard, 1984; Jurkovich, 1972; Mintzberg, 1979; Sharfman and Dean, 1991) is defined in this study as the technological intricacy, market diversity, and geographic concentration of a task environment. Sharfman and Dean (1991) argue that the more geographically concentrated firms are, the less complex an environment is. So environmental complexity is defined as three separate factors: technical sophistication, geographic concentration, and product or market diversity.

The final dimension is munificence or competitive threat (Aldrich, 1979; Dess and Beard, 1984; Pfeffer and Salancik, 1978; Sharfman and Dean, 1991). This dimension is defined as the level of resources available in the industry for firm growth and the level of competition for those resources.

Performance is defined in this study as the ability to grow the firm. Recent empirical evidence suggests that the goal of entrepreneurial firms is to grow (Ensley & Banks, 1992; Siegel et al., 1994; Chandler and Hanks, 1994). Ensley and Banks' work even supports the idea of growth as the intention of top managers of entrepreneurial firms in this study's intended sample (the *inc. 500).* Eighty percent of the entrepreneurs in the Chandler and Hanks (1994) study said that their chief intention was to grow the new venture. Here, growth is defined as sales growth, asset growth and new venture employment growth.

## THE SAMPLE

The sample for both phases of the research was the *inc.* 500 which was a directory of the nation's 500 fastest growing firms. The *inc.* 500 had been shown to have a high number of team-driven entrepreneurial firms (Ensley & Banks, 1992). All members of each entrepreneurial team in the *inc.500* received a personalized letter and questionnaire. To be included as an observation in this study, a response had to be received from two or more members of a firm's entrepreneurial team. Single responses were discarded for this project. Three variables from 30 of the non respondent firms were sampled to assess non-response bias.

## THE SURVEY

The data collection phase of this project was based on a survey which attempted to measure empirically the constructs and relationships shown in Appendix B. The questionnaire was attached to this document in Appendix D. The letter that accompanied the questionnaire was shown

Appendix E. The questionnaire was mailed to the sample for response following Dillman's (1978, p. 181) total design method. A business reply envelope was included with the survey for ease of return. The only response inducement offered respondents was a summary copy of the results. Two weeks after the original mailing of questionnaires a second transmittal letter (Appendix F) and an additional survey were mailed to the non-respondents of the sample. Confidentiality of response was guaranteed by the destruction of the surveys after the data were collected from them. Only the team composition, team behavior, and strategic orientation variables were included in the survey. The environmental variables and performance measures were captured using other data sources. The following sections contain brief discussions of each of the constructs and associated scales and measurements utilized in this study. The reliability and validity coefficients are included in the tables. The reliability and validity coefficients for this study are included in chapter four.

### The Measurement of Entrepreneurial Team Skill Heterogeneity

In the research specific to entrepreneurial teams, no factor was cited as important to firm performance more often than entrepreneurial team skill heterogeneity (Kamm et al., 1990; Roure and Madique, 1986). Gartner (1985) noted that complex ventures require a wide range of skills from the management group. Roure and Madique (1986) implied that the skills and abilities of team members affect firm performance. Yet, skill heterogeneity has seldom been measured in entrepreneurial teams. Furthermore, there was little empirical evidence of the observed relationship between entrepreneurial team skill heterogeneity and cognitive and affective conflict.

The conceptualization and measurement of skills and skill heterogeneity poses special problems for the researcher. What skills should be included in the discovery effort? How should they be chosen? The Katz (1974) skill typology included three skill categories: technical, human, and conceptual. This typology was extended and used as a scale by Herron (1990), and was used as the measurement scale for the skill heterogeneity construct in this project.

Herron (1990) and Katz (1974) provided the rationale for these indicators. In its original form the Katz skill typology was too broad for practical research use. Herron's (1990) extension of Katz's skill typology narrowed the skills under each category to a manageable level for research purposes. Under technical skills, Szilagyi and Schweiger (1984)

**Table 2.1 Measures of Team Skill Heterogeneity**

| **Scale Item** |
| --- |
| My skill in the detailed design of our products/services is: |
| My skill in evaluating the various functions of my organization is: |
| My skill in understanding my industry and the implications of its trends and changes is: |
| My skill in motivating and influencing the behavior of my employees is: |
| My skill in creating relations with and influencing important people outside my organization is: |
| My skill in planning and administering my business' activities is: |
| My skill in discovering *opportunities* to profitably change my business is: |
| The reliability coefficient for this scale is .76. |

*Source:* Herron (1990).

suggested a product/service skill category, an organizational skill category, and an industry skill category. Under the human skills category, leadership skills and networking skills were considered most important. Under conceptual skills, separate categories for administrative skill and entrepreneurial skill were provided.

Herron (1990) utilized the Szilagyi and Schweiger (1984) extended skill typology in his model of new venture performance to create the set of scales shown above. Herron's skill measurement scale had sufficient levels of reliability (reliability coefficient of .76) and validity. Each scale item used a five-point Likert scale ranging from (1) Not Effective, to (5) Extremely Effective. For this research, the standard deviation was used as team-level data points to measure team skill heterogeneity. These variance measures allow for an understanding the range of skills held by members of a particular entrepreneurial team; the greater the difference in the skills among team members, the higher the coefficient of variation or standard deviation.

A second group of indicators intended to measure team skill heterogeneity were also included in the survey. These indicators included major in college, highest degree, and current functional area of the position now held by the respondent. These indicators came directly from Murray's (1989) work on top management team heterogeneity and firm financial performance. Bantel and Jackson (1989) and Jackson et al. (1991) use similar indicators. As can be seen, these indicators were more coarse-grained than the indicators utilized above. There is no previous reliability and validity information available on these measures.

## The Measurement of Conflict

The five items listed in Table 2.2 measure affective conflict and the four items shown in Table 2.3 measure cognitive conflict. These nine items come from a scale originally developed by Jehn (1992) and further refined by Amason and Harrison (1994). Amason and Harrison found the refined conflict scale to have sufficient degrees of reliability and validity. Team members responded to the nine items on a five-point scale ranging from (1) A Great Deal, to (5) None. The reliability and validity of this scale, as well as the other scales used in this project, were measured using a combination of correlation analysis, exploratory factor analysis, and confirmatory factor analysis.

## The Measurement of Strategic Orientation

Strategic orientation was measured in this study by means of the Strategic Orientation of Business Enterprises (STROBE) scale. The STROBE scale, developed by Venkatraman (1989 and 1986) is a twenty-nine item, six dimension scale intended as a measure of business level strategy. In its original form, STROBE has sufficient levels of reliability and validity (inter-item reliability coefficients range come from Venkatraman, 1989). The six dimensions of the STROBE scale are Aggressiveness, Analysis, Defensiveness, Futurity, Proactiveness, and Riskiness. The defensiveness scale is not utilized in this research because it has not been linked empirically or conceptually to an entrepreneurial strategic orientation (Covin and Slevin, 1989; Covin, 1991; Miller, 1983; Miller and Friesen, 1982; Miller and Friesen, 1983; Naman and Slevin, 1993). Table 2.3 lists the scale items used in this research and shows the reliability coefficients for each dimension found in Venkartraman's (1989) study.

## Table 2.2  Measures of Affective Conflict

| Scale Item | Reliability Estimate |
| --- | --- |
| How much emotional conflict is there among the members of your management team? | .49 |
| How much anger is there generally among the members of your top management team in discussions concerning strategic decisions? | .54 |
| How much personal friction is there among top management team members concerning strategic decisions? | .81 |
| How much are personality clashes between team members evident during discussions of strategic decisions? | .55 |
| How much tension is there generally in the top management group during discussions of strategic decisions? | .65 |

*Source:* Amason and Harrison (1994).

## Table 2.3  Measures of Cognitive Conflict

| Scale Item | Reliability Estimate |
| --- | --- |
| How much disagreement is there generally among the members of the top management team over their opinions concerning strategic decisions? | .60 |
| How many disagreements over different ideas about strategic decisions are there generally? | .57 |
| How many differences about the content of strategic decisions does the top management team generally have? | .44 |
| How many differences of opinion are there within the top management group during the discussion of strategic decisions? | .42 |

*Source:* Amason and Harrison (1994).

## Table 2.4  The STROBE Scale

| **Aggressiveness Dimension** | **Reliability coefficient = 0.68** |
|---|---|

This firm tends to sacrifice profitability to gain market share.

This firm tends to cut prices to gain market share.

This firm tends to set prices below competition.

This firm tends to seek market share position at the expense of cash flow and profitability.

| **Analysis Dimension** | **Reliability Coefficient = 0.67** |
|---|---|

This firm emphasizes effective coordination among different functional areas.

Information systems provide support for decision making.

When confronted with a major decision, this firm usually tries to develop solutions through analysis.

This firm uses planning techniques.

This firm uses the outputs of management information and control systems.

This firm uses manpower planning and performance appraisal of senior managers.

| **Futurity Dimension** | **Reliability Coefficient = 0.61** |
|---|---|

Our criteria for resource allocation generally reflects short-term considerations.

We emphasize basic research to provide us with a future competitive edge.

This firm forecasts key indicators of operations.

This firm formally tracks significant general trends.

This firm uses "what-if" analysis on critical issues.

| **Proactiveness Dimension** | **Reliability Coefficient = 0.64** |
|---|---|

This firm constantly seeks new opportunities related to present operations.

This firm is usually the first one to introduce new brands or products in the market.

This firm is constantly on the lookout for businesses that can be acquired.

Competitors generally preempt us by expanding capacity before we do.

Operations in later/larger stages of the product life cycle are strategically eliminated.

**Table 2.4** (*cont.*)

| Riskiness Dimension | Reliability Coefficient = 0.53 |
| --- | --- |
| This firm's operations can be generally characterized as high risk. | |
| This firm seems to adopt a rather conservative view when making major decisions. | |
| New products are approved on a "stage-by-stage" basis rather than with "blanket" approval. | |
| This firm has a tendency to support projects where the expected returns are certain. | |
| Operations of this firm have generally followed the "tried and true" paths. | |

*Source:* Venkatraman (1989).

Team members responded to these twenty-five statements on a five-point Likert scale ranging from (1), Strongly Agree, to (5), Strongly Disagree. The responses to each scale item by the members of each entrepreneurial team member were averaged. Then an average was calculated for each scale dimension. These five dimensions comprised the measures of strategic orientation. The higher the team's mean scores for aggressiveness, analysis, proactiveness, futurity, and riskiness, the more entrepreneurial the firm was considered to be (Covin, 1991; Lumpkin and Dess, 1996; Miller, 1983; Miller and Friesen, 1982, 1983; Miller and Camp, 1985; Mintzberg, 1973). The use of these scales and dimensions agreed with the use of the same or similar scale items by several authors (see Covin, 1991; Covin & Slevin, 1989; Miller, 1983; Miller & Friesen, 1982; Miller and Friesen, 1983). Appendix G contains a table which presents the empirical studies that have utilized these constructs and the purpose of these measures in the study. The table summarized the constructs and shows that the constructs have been in use for some time and that they have been used to measure strategy, strategic orientation, and entrepreneurial orientation.

## THE MEASUREMENT OF THE ENVIRONMENT

Traditionally, measurement of the environment in the new venture research has been limited to entry barriers, industry age, or industry concentration (Sandberg, 1986; McDougall et al., 1992; Sterns et al., 1995).

Dess, Ireland, and Hitt (1990) argued that such a conceptualization of the effects of the environment was incomplete and state that the use of a more comprehensive framework for the measurement of environment was in order. In an effort to address these concerns, a three construct multiple indicant approach was used in this study. The following section discusses how those constructs were chosen, the sources of the data, and how the environmental measures were calculated.

## Choosing Between Objective and Perceptual Environmental Measures

Two types of environmental measures exist in organization theory and strategic management: perceptual and objective. Debate over how best to conceptualize and measure the environment has been fairly constant since Tosi, Aldag, and Storey (1973) argued that the coefficient of variation of industry data could be used to objectively measure environmental volatility. In 1982, Snyder and Glueck found that Tosi et al.'s objective environmental volatility measure was empirically correlated to Duncan's perceptual measure of dynamism, but the battle over whether objective measures of the environment could be constructed raged on. A number of perceptual measures seem to be based on Duncan's (1972) work and Miller and Friesen's (1983) research. These measures basically involved questions about how uncertain executives feel about various aspects of the environment in which their firms exist. Boyd, Dess, and Rasheed (1993) argue that the use of perceptual or objective measures of the environment should rest with the theoretical model on which the study is built. Studies attempting to ascertain the influence of the environment on the performance of the firm should use objective measures of the environment. Those attempting to measure management's propensity to scan the environment should utilize perceptual measures of the environment.

Aldrich (1979) identified six environmental dimensions which could be objectively measured. He argued that objective measures of the environment were necessary because managers were incapable of evaluating the whole of the environment. Dess, Ireland, and Hitt (1990) argued that executives tune themselves into one particular section of the environment and were unable to render assessments of the other parts of the environment. Dess and Beard (1984) created a set of sixteen variables to measure Aldrich's six constructs. After factor analyzing these variables, they retained three constructs and fewer than half of the original variables. The constructs which they kept were dynamism, complexity, and munificence. Appendix H presents the three dimensions have been included in a number of studies (Keats and Hitt, 1988; Lawless and Finich, 1989; McArthur and Nystrom, 1991). Given the empirical support for dynamism, munificence, and complexity, were included in this study as a framework for the conceptualization and measurement of the environment.

Even though a number of studies examined the complexity, dynamism, and munificence of industry environments, there was still some disagreement concerning the measurement of these constructs. Dess and Beard (1984) selected variables to measure each construct based on their factor structures. The problem with this method of variable selection was that it was data driven and not theory driven. Bollen (1989) and Nunnally and Bernstein (1994) were clear that theory should drive the creation and selection of variables. Dess and Beard's (1984) measure of market instability and their measure of technical instability did not load together on one construct and therefore technical instability was dropped from their analysis. Sharfman and Dean (1991) argued that technical and market instability should not load on the same construct but they are a part of the same measure. Sharfman and Dean proposed an alternative set of variables based on theoretical criteria. Dess and Rasheed (1991) argued that their variables may be theoretically less correct but they do offer greater simplicity and ease of use, and were statistically more reliable and valid. In this study statistical ease of use and simplicity was less important than theoretical soundness. Therefore the variables that Sharfman and Dean (1991) identified were utilized in this study with only minor adjustment.

Sharfman and Dean measured technological instability as the average number of patents in an industry. By definition, instability means unpredictable change. The average number of patents failed to measure variability or instability (Dess and Rasheed, 1991). In addition, variability and instability were not the same. Some variability was the product of an identifiable pattern of technological change (Naman and Slevin, 1993; Dess, Ireland, and Hitt, 1990; Wholey and Brittain, 1989). The part of the variance in technological change which was important to this study was the part that was unpredictable, ie., that part of the variance in technology which follows no discernable pattern.

Therefore, a new variable was developed to measure the unpredictable part of technological change in an environment. Sharfman and Dean (1991) argued that market instability should be measured as the standard error of a single regression between revenues in a particular industry (the dependent variable) and time (the independent variable).

The independent variable was a dummy variable which simply uses the year as the data point. If the dependent variable acts predictably then the standard error was small. In that case it would seem that the particular industry shows little market instability.

The use of standard errors as measures of instability is common to both the Dess and Beard (1984) and Sharfman and Dean (1991) studies of environmental measurement. So why could the same not be done with technological instability? Research and development intensity could serve as a measure of technological instability (Tosi et al., 1973; Snyder and Glueck, 1982). As with other instability measures a regression was developed with research and development intensity as the dependent variable and time as the independent variable. Specifically, technological instability in this study was measured as these regression standard errors, divided by the mean of research and development intensity.

## Sources of Data and Calculation of Environmental Measures

The sources of data for the three environmental measures were several governmental sources and the *Compustat Database*. The government sources were the *Census of Manufacturers (1992), Annual Survey of Manufacturers (1995), Annual Service Survey(1995), County Business Patterns(1983-1993), Employment, Hours, and Earnings, (1994-5), Census of Service Industries (1995), Census of Wholesale Trade, Census of Retail Trade, Census of Construction (1992), Annual Wholesale and Retail summary (1996), Annual Construction Survey (1985-1994), Census of Transportation (1992), Motor Freight Transportation and Warehousing Survey (1993), Annual Survey of Communication Industries (1994), Science and Engineering Indicators (1996), and The Statistical Abstract of the United States (1991, 1995).* The technological information was partially available from *Science and Engineering Indicators,* a publication of the National Science Foundation. The percentage of scientists and engineers was available at the Bureau of Labor Statistics world wide web site under special requests. The number of products was derived from eight-digit SIC codes found in the *Industrial Classification Manual (1991)* produced by Dun and Bradstreet information services. Sales and market share data were compiled from the 1990, 1993, and 1996 editions of *Ward's Business Directory, Volume 5,* which ranked firms by sales within a four digit SIC code. Some of the data used in this study were used by special permission of the Bureau of the Census and the National Science Foundation and were not available for general use and were not publishable. They were provided on a one time basis for this project and were used through a cooperative agreement with the University of Central Arkansas, the Bureau of the Census, the Department of Commerce, and the National Science Foundation.

**Dynamism Calculations.** Dynamism in the Sharfman and Dean (1991) framework was measured as the standard errors of three regression slopes. In each case, the independent variable was time. The dependent variables were industry revenues, number of industry employees, and research and development intensity. Each of these variables was regressed with a dummy variable for at least seven years of data. Because more data were available for some industries than others, the industries with the fewest years of data limit the number of years in the calculations. This was because using standard errors calculated with different numbers of years would create comparability problems between industries. The years of 1985-1994 was used to calculate the employment standard error. The years 1988-1995 was used to calculate the revenues standard error. The years of 1988-1996 was used to calculated the standard error of research and development intensity. The standard error of the regressions divided by the mean of the respective variable was the measure of instability. Z scores were used to ensure that all variables were on the same metric. The calculation of the dynamism variable was as follows: Formula One

$$\text{Dynamism} = Z(\text{MI+NEI}) + Z(\text{TI}) + 10$$

Where MI is equal to market instability, NEI is equal to number of employees instability, and TI is equal to technological instability. (The ten added to the end of the equation was to ensure that the measures were positive. The limits of these measures were zero to positive infinity).

**Complexity Calculations.** Sharfman and Dean (1991) argued that industry complexity had three traits: geographic complexity, technical complexity, and element complexity. Geographic complexity (GC) was measured using two variables. The first was the geographic concentration of the number of firms. Which was calculated as the sum of the number of industry firms in a census division divided by the total number of firms in that census division squared divided by the sum of the number of industry firms in a census division quantity squared. The same technique was used with the geographic concentration of the number of employees.

Technical complexity (TC) was measured as the employment of scientists and engineers as a percentage of total employment in an industry. Element or product complexity (EPC) was measured as the number of eight digit SIC codes in an industry (within a four digit industry level). The calculation of the complexity measure was: Formula Two

$$\text{Complexity} = Z(\text{EPC}) + Z(\text{TC}) - Z(\text{GC}) + 10$$

Where EPC is equal to the number different products in an industry, TC is equal to technical complexity, and GC is equal to geographic complexity. Geographic complexity is calculated as GCNF (geographic concentration of the number of firms) + GCNE (geographic concentration of the number of employees). Z scores are used to ensure that all measures were on the same metric. The constant was added to assure that the measures stay within the bound of zero to positive infinity.

**Competitive Threat.** Competitive threat was principally the same theoretical construct as environmental munificence but it includes a competitive dimension. Sharfman and Dean (1991) argued that not only is the level of available resources in an environment important but that the rivalry for those resources was also important. Not only did Sharfman and Dean (1991) include traditional munificence variables from Dess and Beard (1984) but they also included measures of competitive rivalry. Munificence was measured as the slope of the regression function derived in the calculation of the dynamism calculation above divided by the mean of that variable. Competitive rivalry was measured two ways. The first measure of competitive rivalry was the eight-firm concentration ratio (this was a common measure of industry concentration, see Bain and Qualls, 1987, for a complete discussion of the use of this measure). The second measure of competitiveness was average market share change. Klein (1977, p 56) showed that "substantial changes in market share indicate high levels of competition." The calculation of the competitive threat measure was as follows: Formula Three

$$\text{Competitive Threat} = Z(\sqrt{(\text{NF} \times \text{MSC})/(10.05 + \text{MUN})})$$

Where NF was equal to the number of firms in the eight firm concentration ratio over the years 1990, 1993, and 1996, MSC was equal to the average market share change over the years 1990 and 1996, and MUN was equal to munificence. Munificence was calculated as RM + NEM, where RM was equal to revenues munificence and NEM was equal to number of employees munificence. Z scores were employed to ensure that the variables were all on the same metric. The constant was added to the denominator of the equation to ensure that the scale ranged from zero to positive infinity as it was assumed that a negative competitive threat could not exist.

Accurately measuring the environment was an important aspect of strategic management research and was critical to future studies concerning the link between the environment, strategy, and performance (Dess et al., 1990). Sharfman and Dean's (1991) framework for measuring the environment was the "best" effort thus far in the search for environmental dimensions and measures. As Dess and Beard (1991) say Sharfman and Dean's work was theoretically "the most correct set of environmental measures." They sacrifice simplicity and ease of statistical use but they gained theoretical soundness. Sharfman and Dean (1991) found empirical support for content, construct, predictive, and nomological validity of their measures. Sharfman and Dean (1991) specifically showed that their measures were more valid than were those suggested by Dess and Beard (1984) because they confirm the theoretical models of the role of environment in organizations. Dess and Beard (1991) did criticize Sharfman and Dean (1991) for not statistically testing the reliability of their measures and assuming the reliability of their measures on theoretical terms.

## THE MEASUREMENT OF FINANCIAL PERFORMANCE

The five financial performance measures chosen are based on several works (Keats & Hitt, 1988; McGuire, Schneweis, & Hill, 1986; Schaefer, Kenny, & Bost, 1990). Growth is often cited as an objective of entrepreneurial firms. Sales growth rates for last year and an average sales growth rate over the past five years will be utilized in the analysis. In addition, the growth rate in the number of employees, an often cited side effect of entrepreneurial firms on the economy, will be utilized. In addition the new ventures in this sample were placed into categories of profitability levels but this may not be a meaningful measure of performance in entrepreneurial firms given the growth objectives of most new ventures. A recent study by Chandler and Hanks (1993) found that the great majority of entrepreneurs have growth concerns that far outweigh their concerns about profitability. Brush and Vanderwerf (1992) found in a review of 34 empirical studies in entrepreneurship that employee and sales growth were the most common variables used. These studies support the use of growth as a measure of new venture performance.

Sources of performance data include *Inc.* magazine, as well as Dun and Bradstreet's Market Identifiers database. Survey data were not used in order to allow the study to lessen the effects of common method variance and to allow the respondents to concentrate their attention on the entrepreneurial team dynamics variables and dimensions. The questionnaires were coded with an identification number for the purpose defraying additional mailing costs and to allow results to be matched with appropriate financial information. Confidentiality of the respondents was protected.

## THE CALCULATION OF INTERACTION TERMS

To operationalize the strategy-environment interaction the mean of each of the strategy dimensions was multiplied by the three environmental variables. The product of these multiplications became the interaction variables. Fifteen interaction variables were calculated in this way.

## SUMMARY OF SCALES TO BE UTILIZED

With the exception of some of the measures of skill heterogeneity and part of the measures of the environment, all of the scales utilized in this study have been tested for reliability and validity. Appendix I contains a summary table of the scales utilized in this project. The conflict scale(s) and the STROBE scale were tested using confirmatory factor analysis, and the skill scale has been tested with a combination of exploratory factor analysis, and correlation analysis. Only the skill heterogeneity indicators from Murray (1989), utilized here, have no reported reliability or validity indices.

Reliability and validity of the performance indicators were another issue. These indicators were seldom tested for reliability and validity and tend to fail such tests when they were tested. For this reason, the technique used by Schaefer et al. (1990) was utilized in this research for the selection of performance indicators. They argued that many different performance measures should be utilized and that the performance measures used in a study should make sense, given the sample frame and the characteristics of that sample frame. As a theoretical guide Brush and Vanderwerf's (1992) study of 34 empirical studies in entrepreneurship found that sales and employee growth were the most commonly utilized new performance variables. They were employed in this study.

In sum, no new scales were constructed for this study. Only existing scales, most with known reliability and validity coefficients, were employed. This allowed the researcher to concentrate on the relationships between the constructs rather than the conceptualization and measurement of the constructs. It is the relationships between the constructs which were the crux of this project.

## STATISTICAL ASSESSMENT OF THE HYPOTHESES

Cronbach's *Alpha* coefficient and common factor analysis were used to assess reliability, and construct validity of all scales and measures. The reliability and validity of the environmental measures was assessed by comparing the results of the work of Sharfman and Dean (1991) and the findings in this project. Internal and between statistical structures were checked by factor analysis (Nunnally and Bernstien, 1994).

The chief statistical tool used for testing the hypotheses was hierarchial regression analysis. Hierarchial regression was a analytic strategy by which variable(s) enter the model depending on their theoretical importance. Ordinary least squares was used to test each of the hierarchial steps. Hierarchial regression was used here for several reasons. First, it had perhaps the most rigorous set of tests of assumptions of any multivariate statistical tool (Belsley, Kuh, and Welsch, 1980). Second, it allowed the researcher to test the influence of several variables at the same time.

Hypothesis One was tested with a series of regressions between the indicators of skill heterogeneity as independent variables and the indicators of conflict as dependent variables. These tests were conducted twice, once with the scales developed by Herron (1990) and a second time with the skill heterogeneity measures used by Bantel and Jackson (1989) and Murray (1989). Confirmation of the hypothesis occurred when regressions between the skill heterogeneity variables were significant predictors of the level of both types of conflict in the entrepreneurial firm. Significance tests on the regression coefficients for each variable allowed the researcher to understand the importance of each skill variable on the level of conflict. The signs of the regression coefficients should be positive and significant. *R*-square was used to determine the total amount of variance explained.

Statistical assessment of Hypothesis Two included regressions between the variables that measure cognitive conflict as independent variables and the variables measuring affective conflict as dependent variables in a series. Cognitive conflict and strategic orientation were treated in a similar manner. For this hypothesis to be confirmed the signs of the regression coefficients would have to be positive. The *F-ratio* would be significant on all of the regressions. The significance tests on the regression weights indicated which of the variables contribute to the model.

The third set of hypotheses argued that strategic orientation was linked to new venture performance. These links were tested again using a set of regressions. The five strategic orientation variables were regressed against the six indicators of firm performance. Significant regressions were a sign of a link between strategic orientation and new venture performance. Support for the third set of hypotheses means not only significant regression models but positive signs on regression coefficients as well.

Hypothesis four posed a link between the environmental variables and new venture performance. These links again were tested with regressions. The three environmental variables were regressed against the six indicators of firm performance. Significant regressions with positive regression coefficients were a sign of a link between the environment and new venture performance.

Hypothesis five posits that the interaction of strategic orientation and environment will positively affect the performance of new ventures. Regressions were conducted on the interaction variables as independents and new venture performance variables as dependent variables. Significant regressions with positive regression coefficients indicated support for hypothesis four.

CHAPTER 4

# Results of the Study

The purpose of this chapter is to report the findings of this study. The results are reported in the following manner. The first section contains a discussion of the response rate and non-response bias. Non-response bias was tested with the variables used to define respondents as members of the entrepreneurial team. The second section presents a short description of the sample used in this research. The third section discusses the reliability and validity of the data gathered and the scales used. The fourth section is a discussion of the statistical analysis technique and the testing of the assumptions of that technique. The fifth section describes the method by which the skill scale and conflict variables were collapsed into dimensional indicators. The final section is broken into five parts, one section for each of the five hypotheses, and presents the findings.

## RESPONSE RATE

In an effort to gather data on teams of entrepreneurs, all of the *inc. 500* were utilized as the sample for this study. The *inc. 500* is a group of firms which are independently owned and were among the fastest growing firms in the U.S. The December 1994 list of firms is used in this study. Each of the 1203 officers of these 500 firms received a personalized transmittal letter and individually numbered questionnaire. All questionnaires were coded to reduce mailing costs and to link the response to environmental and performance data. Of the 1203 questionnaires mailed, 322 usable responses were returned. Usable responses were received from 214 firms. Because 56 firms were either out of business or harvested by their entrepreneurs during the time of the study, 167 officers were dropped from the calculation of the response rate. These firms either self-reported that they were purchased, the purchase of the firm was published in *inc.,* or the purchase was a recent posting on the Dun and Bradstreet data base. Given these adjustments, the effective officer response rate was 31.4 percent. The effective firm response rate was 48.2 percent. The effective response rate deducts firms or officers from the total sample that could not respond because they no longer existed, had left the firm, or were no longer at the correct address (Dillman, 1978). This lowered the total sample to 1036 officers and 444 firms.

In order for respondents to be considered a member of the entrepreneurial team they had to meet at least two of three criteria listed in chapter three; i.e., they had to be founders, equity stake holders, and/or involved in the strategic decision making of the firm. In total, 88 teams of entrepreneurs and 196 individual entrepreneurs were included in the sample used in the analysis of this study. Teams ranged in size from two to four.

## TESTING NON-RESPONSE BIAS

Since the criteria for a respondent to be selected into the team were so important, the criterion variables were used as the basis for a test of non-response bias. A random sample of 50 non-respondents were selected and contacted by phone. Five variables were gathered: team size, how often new strategic plans were developed, involvement in strategic decisions, founder status, and equity status. *T-tests* on these five variables all yielded non-significant probability values ranging from .39-.84. Based on these tests there was no evidence of non-response bias. Table 4.1 presents the non-response bias statistics.

**Table 4.1 Non-response Bias Results**

| Item | *t*-value | *p*-level |
|---|---|---|
| Team Size | .23 | .82 |
| How often new strategic plans are developed | .20 | .84 |
| Involvement in strategic decisions | .74 | .55 |
| Founder Status | .85 | .39 |
| Equity Status | .62 | .54 |

## DESCRIPTION OF THE SAMPLE

This section contains a short demographic description of the sample used in this study. Approximately 90 percent of the sample were male. The average age of the respondents was 38.4 years. 70 percent were founders and 74 percent held at least 10 percent of the equity of the firms they were involved with. Almost 90 percent considered themselves entrepreneurs. Only 40 percent had been involved in a new venture previously. Eight percent held high school diplomas, four percent held associates degrees, 50 percent held bachelors degrees, 33 percent held masters degrees, and almost 5 percent held doctoral degrees. 32 percent majored in business, 6 percent in accounting, and 13.2 in engineering. Other majors included english, history, nursing, medical technology, sports management, law, and kinesiology (all of which these exceeded five percent of the total of all majors).

The firms in this sample grew at an annual average of 1,664 percent over the last five years. The five year sales growth rate range was 524 percent to 11,385 percent. The standard deviation of the five year sales growth rate was 2,065 percent. The industries covered by the sample included a range from SIC code 1521 to 8713. In all 55 industries were occupied by the 88 firms in this sample. The average age of the firms in this sample at the time of the study was 4.6 years.

## RELIABILITY AND VALIDITY

This section reports reliability and validity indices associated with the scale items used in this study. The process for the assessment of reliability and validity was two fold. First, a factor analysis of the dimensions was conducted and those items with low loadings, cross loadings, or no loadings were eliminated from the analysis. Second, an assessment of the reduced scales was conducted. In total ten items were eliminated from the analysis. No construct was left with less than three indicators as suggested by Bollen (1989). The first part of this section discusses the items that were eliminated, the dimension they were eliminated from, and the reason for the item's elimination. The second section discusses and presents the reduced factor analysis and discusses the construct validity of the purified scales. The final part of this section discusses and presents the reliability coefficients related to the dimensions in this study.

## Scale Purification

The factor analysis demonstrated that eight of the items in the theoretical model did not behave as expected. Therefore eight items were eliminated from the testing of hypotheses because they lowered or did not add to the internal statistical structure of the dimensions (Nunnally and Bernstein, 1994). Items were trimmed from the analysis for two main reasons: items cross loaded between two or more dimensions or the item failed to significantly load on any dimension. Loadings were considered significant at the + .35 level (Hair, Tathum, Anderson, and Black, 1995). At least one item was eliminated from each of the strategy dimensions. Two items were eliminated from the futurity and proactivness dimensions. In addition, two items were eliminated from the skill scale. Table 4.2 contains the items eliminated, the theoretical construct which they were eliminated from, and the reason they were eliminated from the analysis.

The justification for the elimination of these items was simple and best captured by Loehlin (1992). Loehlin argued that some items simply fail to measure the constructs to which they were theoretically tied. These items tend to measure little variance and therefore should be eliminated (Loehlin, 1992). Other items may represent constructs they were not intended to measure and therefore cause model mis-specification problems. When there was evidence that either of these conditions existed in this study the items were eliminated. The large number of indicators for each construct gave the researcher the freedom to eliminate "unruly" scale items and still have sufficient numbers of indicators for each construct (Bollen, 1989). Therefore items that cross-loaded or failed to load were eliminated from the analysis.

## Construct Validity

Table 4.3 shows a series of factor analyses which were the basis for the assessment of construct validity in this project. Factor analysis was helpful in determining construct validity by illuminating the constructs' internal statistical structure and measuring the cross statistical structures between constructs (Nunnnally and Bernstein, 1994). Most of the scales in this study measure multiple constructs and therefore both the internal statistical structure and the cross structures of the constructs can be tested. However, the skill scale had only one construct and therefore only the internal statistical structure can be tested. Again, only loadings greater than or less than +.35 were considered significant (Hair, Tathum, Anderson, and Black, 1995).

**Table 4.2  Items Eliminated from the Analysis Through Scale Purification**

| Item | Construct | Reason |
|---|---|---|
| This firm tends to set prices below the competition. | Aggressiveness | Cross-loaded |
| This firm uses manpower planning and performance appraisal of senior managers. | Defensiveness | No loading |
| This firm has engaged in significant modifications to its manufacturing technology. | Analysis | Cross-loaded |
| Our criteria for resource allocation generally reflects short-term considerations. | Futurity | No loading |
| We emphasize basic research to provide us with a future competitive edge. | Futurity | Cross-loaded |
| Operations in the later stages of the product life cycle are strategically eliminated. | Proactivness | Cross-loaded |
| Competitors generally preempt this firm expanding capacity before this firm does. | Proactivness | Cross-loaded |
| This firm's operations can be generally characterized as high-risk. | Riskiness | Cross-loaded |
| My skill in the detailed design of our products/services is: | Skill Scale | Cross-loaded |
| My skill in planning and administering our business' activities is: | Skill Scale | Cross-loaded |

## Table 4.3  Assessment of Construct Validity

**Part One: Assessment of the Skill Scale (Internal Statistical Structure Only)**
**Rotated Factor Loadings (Varimax Rotation)**

**Eigenvalue Factor One: 2.6555**      **Next highest eigenvalue: .8266**

| Item | Factor 1 |
|------|----------|
| Function | 0.7442 |
| Industry | 0.7535 |
| Behavior | 0.6347 |
| Relationships | 0.7591 |
| Opportunities | 0.7450 |

**Part Two: Assessment of the Conflict Scale, Construct Validity**
**Rotated Factor Loadings (Varimax Rotation)**

**Eigenvalue for Affective Conflict: 3.38**     **Eigenvalue for Cognitive Conflict: 2.75**
**Next Highest Eigenvalue: 0.5880**

| Item | Factors | |
|------|-----------|-----------|
|      | **Affective** | **Cognitive** |
| Emotion | **0.6548** | 0.3242 |
| Anger | **0.7990** | 0.2599 |
| Friction | **0.8262** | 0.2617 |
| Clashes | **0.7932** | 0.2881 |
| Tension | **0.7637** | 0.3277 |
| Disagree | 0.3370 | **0.7595** |
| Many | 0.3131 | **0.7998** |
| Content | 0.2118 | **0.7774** |
| Opinion | 0.3255 | **0.7559** |

**Table 4.3** (*cont.*)

---

**Part Three: Assessment of the Reduced STROBE scale for Construct Validity Rotated Factor Loadings (Varimax Rotation)**

---

| | Factor | | | | | |
|---|---|---|---|---|---|---|
| **ITEM** | **Defensive** | **Riskiness** | **Aggressive** | **Analysis** | **Proact.** | **Futurity** |
| Mkt Share | 0.0792 | 0.1164 | **-.8620** | 0.0662 | 0.0014 | 0.0986 |
| Prices | 0.0225 | -.1046 | **-.7705** | 0.0663 | -.0535 | 0.1094 |
| Expense | 0.1269 | 0.1269 | **-.7950** | 0.2033 | 0.0143 | 0.1103 |
| Coordinat. | -.0647 | 0.0332 | 0.2389 | **-.6433** | 0.1584 | -.0269 |
| Informat. | 0.0199 | -.0468 | 0.0775 | **-.7924** | 0.0913 | -.1242 |
| Solutions | -.2494 | -.1178 | 0.0961 | **-.6548** | 0.1120 | -.1861 |
| Planning | **-.4287** | -.0786 | 0.1313 | **-.5229** | 0.0649 | -.2479 |
| Outputs | -.1941 | -.0594 | -.0713 | **-.6840** | -.0509 | -.3537 |
| Perform | **-.4409** | -.0863 | 0.0819 | -.2893 | 0.0833 | -.3132 |
| Product | **-.7801** | 0.0461 | 0.0846 | -.1187 | -.1049 | -.1666 |
| Quality | **0.7615** | -.0830 | 0.0695 | -.0972 | 0.1527 | -.0613 |
| Forecasts | -.1610 | 0.0439 | 0.0663 | -.1936 | 0.0627 | **-.7881** |
| Trends | -.0995 | 0.0516 | 0.1459 | -.2100 | 0.0474 | **-.8053** |
| What-If | -.1840 | -.0976 | 0.2138 | -.2041 | 0.2566 | **-.5862** |
| Newopport | -.0522 | -.0021 | 0.0599 | -.2167 | **0.7174** | -.0827 |
| First | -.1524 | 0.1847 | -.0205 | -.1940 | **0.6281** | 0.0568 |
| Acquired | 0.1042 | 0.0077 | -.0041 | 0.1506 | **0.6527** | -.3249 |
| Conservat. | 0.0788 | **-.6881** | 0.1888 | -.0097 | -.1809 | 0.0769 |
| Blanket | -.2614 | **-.5660** | -.0680 | -.0139 | 0.1660 | 0.0469 |
| CertainRt | 0.0867 | **-.6222** | 0.0635 | -.2974 | 0.0508 | 0.0149 |
| Tried & Tru. | -.0803 | **-.7281** | -.0551 | 0.0708 | -.2158 | -.1331 |

All of the reduced scales demonstrated sufficient internal and between statistical structures. The next section presents the reliability coefficients of the reduced scales.

## Assessment of Reliability of the Reduced Scales

The assessment of reliability was conducted after factor analysis was used to purify the scales and establish construct validity. Inter-item reliability was tested using Cronbach's Alpha. Alpha was an intra-class correlation measure that was an actual measure of inter-item reliability. An Alpha above .70 was considered satisfactory for all but exploratory studies. An Alpha of .60 would for exploratory work (Nunnally and Bernstein, 1994).

The reliability coefficients in Table 4.4 contained acceptable reliability scores for all constructs. Both of the conflict scales were in excess of the .70 boundary set by Nunnally and Bernstein (1994). The skill scale and three of the six strategy dimensions were also in excess of the .70 rule of thumb. The scales riskiness and proactivness were close to .70 while the construct called defensiveness was closer to .60. Hair, Tathum, Anderson, and Black (1994) note that some flexibility exists for the .70 boundary in exploratory research. This project was exploratory and the violation of the boundary was quite small.

**Table 4.4  Reliability Indices of the Reduced Scales**

| Construct | Number of Items Used | Alpha |
|---|---|---|
| Skill heterogeneity | Five | .78 |
| Affective Conflict | Five | .88 |
| Cognitive Conflict | Four | .85 |
| Riskiness | Four | .68 |
| Proactivness | Three | .65 |
| Aggressiveness | Three | .79 |
| Analysis | Five | .79 |
| Futurity | Three | .76 |
| Defensiveness | Three | .62 |

## ANALYSIS TECHNIQUE

The choice of statistical analysis technique for this study was hierarchial regression. Hierarchial regression was really a choice of analytic strategies as much as a choice of a statistical tool. Hierarchial regression allowed for the testing of variables or groups of variables in their theoretical order of importance. Because of the large number of independent variables in this theoretical model a technique that offered the ability to look at parts of the theory and test the significance of the increase in *r*-square was important. Hierarchial regression was a series of regressions each adding an additional segment of the theoretical model. Tests were then conducted to discover if additional segments of the theory added significant amounts of explained variance (Cohen and Cohen, 1983). Hierarchial regression specifically fits the hypotheses because it allowed for the testing of the links in the theoretical model and illuminates specific variables which were of the greatest importance to that particular link.

To understand the hierarchial strategy fully, a discussion of multiple regression is also necessary. Multiple regression is a dependence technique that can be used to predict dependent variables or create statistical linkages between dependent and independent variables. Regression utilizes metric or non-metric dependent variables but should employ a metric dependent variable. The ordinary least squares version of regression was utilized in this study. Regression has four major assumptions; autocorrelation, normality of error terms, absence of multicollinearity, and homoscedasticity. The assumptions were tested and presented in the next section.

### Testing of Regression Assumptions and Influential Observations

Four assumptions were important in regression analysis: multicollinearity, autocorrelation, homoscedasticity, and normality of error terms. Belsley, Kuh, and Welsch (1980) suggested the following method for assessing multicollinearity: condition indexes greater than 30 indicated the existence of mulitcollinearity. If condition indexes existed in excess of thirty the researcher would then look for the source of the collinearity. Variance decompositions greater than .5 shows between which of the variables the collinearity exists. Since none of the condition indexes in this study exceeded 30 there was no evidence that multicollinearity was at a level high enough to influence the results of the regression analyses. The Durbin-Watson statistic (Neter, Wasserman, and Kutner, 1990) was used to test autocorrelation. Of the many regressions conducted not one was found to have significant levels of autocorrelation. Heteroscedasticity was tested using the White test (White, 1980). None of the White tests conducted showed any evidence of inequality of variances. The normality of error terms was tested by using normal probability plots. The plots appeared to be near normal. The variances were equal, collinearity was not a problem, autocorrelation was non-significant, and the error terms appeared to be close to normal. Overall, the data did not appear to violate any of the major assumptions of regression analysis.

Influential observations or outliers were observed in some of the regression analyses in this study. In order to test their level of influence, observations with significant *R-students* and standardized residuals greater than 2.0 were dropped from the analysis. The regressions with and without these observations were compared in an effort to find differences. No observation was influential enough to change the outcomes of the analysis so all observations were retained.

## THE CREATION OF TEAM LEVEL VARIABLES

This section discusses the method by which the skill scale and conflict scales were collapsed into single variables and the traditional measures of skill heterogeneity were transformed into indices. The Katz (1974) skill scale was used in this study as an attempt to measure skill heterogeneity or skill difference. To create the variable skill heterogeneity, the skills of individual team members were measured first. Individual means on the reduced five item skill scale were then calculated. Team skill heterogeneity was then measured as the standard deviation of the individual skill scale averages.

The variables of heterogeneity of educational degree, major in highest degree, and functional area were all developed using Blau's categorical index (1977). Blau's index used the proportion of the team with a certain characteristic, such as a certain major in college, and sums the squared proportions and subtracts the sum from one. This method has been used by Murray (1989) and Bantel and Jackson (1991). The equation for Blau's categorical index was:

$$\text{Blau's Categorical Index} = 1 - \sum pi^2$$

where pi was the proportion of the population in a given group. This calculation resulted in a measure of heterogeneity and its complement was homogeneity.

Since the quantity of each type of conflict within these entrepreneurial teams was the important issue, it was important that the collapsing of the items measuring affective and cognitive conflict retain as much of their original variance as possible. Therefore a process of summing affective and cognitive conflict items was used. The conflict items were measured on Likert-type scales. Team means of each of the conflict indicators were calculated. The means were then added together to create conflict measures. The team averages of the indicators of affective conflict, five items, were summed as were the team averages of the four cognitive conflict items. These two variables were used to measure the amount of each type of conflict within the entrepreneurial team.

## TESTING OF THE THEORETICAL MODEL

The following sections contain results and tables of the hypotheses tests in this study. The hypotheses are presented in numerical order. Table(s) and short discussions are presented with each set of findings. The final section of this chapter contains a hierarchial test of the full model. Although this analysis is not a direct test of a particular hypothesis, it is a test of the significance of the overall model.

## FINDINGS ON THE LINK BETWEEN SKILL HETEROGENEITY AND CONFLICT

Hypotheses One "A" and "B" were tested using Hierarchial Regression. The analytical strategy was simple. Following the theoretical model the first independent variable included in the model was skill heterogeneity as measured by the skill scale. To control for heterogeneity differences caused by different sizes of teams, the number of members in the team was included with skill heterogeneity as a control variable. The second set of independent variables included in the hierarchy were the traditional demographically oriented skill variables which include difference in degree in college, differences in the majors in the highest degree, and differences team members functional areas. Tables 4.5 and 4.6 present the outcomes of these regressions.

There was no evidence from this study which supports a link between skill heterogeneity and affective conflict. None of the regressions presented in Table 4.5 were significant. Therefore there was no support for Hypothesis One "A." Table 4.6 presents the findings of the link between skill heterogeneity and cognitive conflict. Following the theoretical model, the order for entry into the hierarchy was skill hetero-

**Table 4.5  Test of Hypothesis One "A": The Link Between Skill Heterogeneity and Affective Conflict**

| Variables | Model 1 *betas* | Model 2 *betas* |
|---|---|---|
| **Affective Conflict (Dependent)** | | |
| Skill Heterogeneity | 0.50 | 0.52 |
| Team Size | 0.06 | 0.03 |
| Degree Index | | -.55 |
| Major Index | | 1.06 |
| Function Index | | -.103 |
| $R^2$ | 0.014 | 0.02 |
| $F$ | 1.16 | 0.40 |
| Change $R^2$ | | 0.06 |
| Change $F$ | | -.76 |

N=88; *$p$<.01; **$p$<.05; ***$p$<.10

**Table 4.6  Test of Hypothesis One "B": The Link Between Skill Heterogeneity and Cognitive Conflict**

| Variables | Model 1 *betas* | Model 2 *betas* |
|---|---|---|
| **Cognitive Conflict (Dependent)** | | |
| Skill Heterogeneity | 0.25 | 0.24 |
| Team Size | 0.18 | 0.16 |
| Degree | | 0.67 |
| Major | | 0.74 |
| Function | | -.71 |
| $R^2$ | 0.0087 | 0.026 |
| $F$ | 0.37 | 0.53 |
| Change $R^2$ | | 0.017 |
| Change $F$ | | 0.16 |

N=88; *$p$<.01; **$p$<.05; ***$p$<.10

geneity and team size and then the educational and functional background variables.

No empirical support exists for Hypothesis One "B." None of the three levels of the hierarchy were found to be significant. Simply, no support was found for a link between skill heterogeneity and either type of conflict.

## TESTING THE LINK BETWEEN COGNITIVE CONFLICT, AFFECTIVE CONFLICT, AND STRATEGIC ORIENTATION

The link between cognitive conflict and affective conflict was tested using regression. Since it was impossible to develop a hierarchy from a theoretical standpoint the traditional regression approach was used. Table 4.7 contains the outcomes of the regression between affective and cognitive conflict.

Since the regression was significant with an *r*-square of .54 Hypothesis Two "A" was supported. Overall, the level of cognitive conflict explains about half of the level of affective conflict. The relationship was positive. Disagreements about strategic decisions increased affective conflict within these entrepreneurial teams.

**Table 4.7 Results of Regression Analyses Between Cognitive and Affective Conflict**

| Dependent: Affective Conflict | |
| --- | --- |
| Independents | *betas* |
| Cognitive Conflict | .98* |
| $R^2$ | 0.54 |
| F | 98.68* |

N=88; *$p<.01$; **$p<.05$; ***$p<.10$

## THE LINK BETWEEN CONFLICT AND STRATEGIC ORIENTATION

This section presents the findings on the link between both types of conflict and strategic orientation. Table 4.8 contains the results of Hypothesis Two "B" and Table 4.9 contains the results of Hypothesis Two "C." The results of testing Hypothesis Two "D" are presented in Table 4.10. Since it is theoretically difficult to set a hierarchial strategy for these regressions, the traditional regression approach is used.

Of the five regressions calculated on the relationship between cognitive conflict and strategic orientation, only one was found to be significant. There does appear to be a link between the level of cognitive conflict level and the aggressiveness of the firms' strategic posture. That relationship though only explains 15 percent of the total variation in strategic aggressiveness. Note that cognitive conflict had a positive effect

**Table 4.8  Results of Regression Analyses on Cognitive Conflict and Strategic Orientation**

| Dependents: | Proact. | Risk | Analysis | Futurity | Agres. |
|---|---|---|---|---|---|
| Independents | *betas* | *betas* | *betas* | *betas* | *betas* |
| Cognitive Conflict | -.005 | -.011 | -.038 | -.015 | 0.168* |
| $R^2$ | 0.004 | 0.002 | 0.023 | 0.026 | 0.15 |
| *F* | 0.03 | 0.13 | 1.99 | 0.22 | 17.92* |

N=88; *$p<.01$; **$p<.05$; ***$p<.10$

**Table 4.9  Results of Regression Analyses on Affective Conflict and Strategic Orientation**

| Dependents: | Proact. | Risk | Analysis | Futurity | Agres. |
|---|---|---|---|---|---|
| Independents | *betas* | *betas* | *betas* | *betas* | *betas* |
| Affective Conflict | -.036*** | 0.002 | -.048** | -.045*** | 0.12* |
| $R^2$ | 0.084 | 0.001 | 0.081 | 0.064 | 0.13 |
| *F* | 3.13*** | 0.01 | 5.89** | 3.49*** | 12.52* |

N=88; *$p<.01$; **$p<.05$; ***$p<.10$

on strategic aggressiveness. Though this finding was important and should not be dismissed, it was not sufficient within itself to support the hypothesis. Therefore only weak support for this hypothesis existed.

The regressions in Table 4.9 were evidence that affective conflict affects strategic choice in these new ventures. First, affective conflict was positively linked to strategic aggressiveness. Three of the other four regressions were also significant, but the sign on the parameter estimates was negative. Affective conflict had negative effects on proactivness, analysis, and futurity. These results support for Hypothesis Two "C."

## THE LINK BETWEEN AFFECTIVE CONFLICT AND PERFORMANCE

Hypothesis Two "D" proposed a direct link between affective conflict and performance. Since there is significant disagreement about the role of affective conflict in top management groups, this hypothesis was proposed as exploratory. The findings of these regression analyses is presented in Table 4.10.

There is no support for Hypothesis Two "D." As can be seen in Table 4.10 not a single regression is significant. A direct link between affective conflict and firm performance cannot be supported by this research. In the next section the findings concerning the link between strategic orientation and performance are discussed.

**Table 4.10  Results of Regression Analyses on Affective Conflict and Firm Performance**

| Dependents: | Growth | Sales93 | Profit | Employ93 | Salgrper | Employ Growth |
|---|---|---|---|---|---|---|
| Independent | *betas* | *betas* | *betas* | *betas* | *betas* | *betas* |
| Affective Conflict | 2.07 | -301.7 | -.02 | 2.27 | -3.13 | 2.61 |
| $R^2$ | 0.009 | 0.017 | 0.022 | 0.024 | 0.088 | 0.043 |
| F | *0.026* | *0.090* | *0.174* | *0.203* | *0.760* | *0.371* |

N=88; *$p<.01$; **$p<.05$; ***$p<.10$

## EXPLORING THE STRATEGY-PERFORMANCE LINK

Table 4.11 presents a series of hierarchial regressions on the links between strategic orientation and performance. Hypothesis Three proposes that a link should exist between a firm's choice of strategy and performance. Specifically, the researcher proposed that the choice of a more entrepreneurial strategic orientation should lead to higher levels of performance. The performance variables include sales growth, employee growth, profitability, sales, number of employees, and sales growth per employee. All of these variables have been utilized in the past as measures of firm financial performance.

The hierarchy developed here is based on those variables traditionally included as measures of entrepreneurial orientation and therefore on the theoretical model from this study. Since proactivness and riskiness have traditionally been included in measures of strategic orientation in entrepreneurial firms, they took the highest position in the hierarchy and were included first. The other four strategic orientation variables are included in subsequent regressions. Table 4.11 presents those findings.

**Table 4.11  Test of Hypothesis Three:
The Link Between Strategic Orientation and Performance**

| Variables | Model 1 *betas* | Model 2 *betas* |
|---|---|---|
| **Sales Growth (Dependent)** | | |
| Riskiness | 473.1 | 943.01** |
| Proactivness | -427.2 | -1024.4** |
| Aggressiveness | | -247.4 |
| Analysis | | 811.59 |
| Defensiveness | | -338.32 |
| Futurity | | 251.24 |
| $R^2$ | 0.0216 | 0.1313 |
| $F$ | 0.927 | 2.016*** |
| Change $R^2$ | | 0.1097** |
| Change $F$ | | 1.089 |

N=88; *$p<.01$; **$p<.05$; ***$p<.10$

**Table 4.11** *(cont.)*

**Test of Hypothesis Three: Part Two**
**The Link Between Strategic Orientation and Performance**

| Variables | Model 1 *betas* | Model 2 *betas* |
|---|---|---|
| **Sales for 1993 (Dependent)** | | |
| Riskiness | 10201** | 11128** |
| Proactivness | -8344.5 | -12519** |
| Aggressiveness | | 4983.8 |
| Analysis | | 9032.8 |
| Defensiveness | | -4139.4 |
| Futurity | | 1262.8 |
| $R^2$ | 0.0585 | 0.1161 |
| $F$ | 2.612*** | 1.751 |
| Change $R^2$ | | 0.058 |
| Change $F$ | | -.861 |

N=88; *$p<.01$; **$p<.05$; ***$p<.10$

**Test of Hypothesis Three: Part Three**
**The Link Between Strategic Orientation and Performance**

| Variables | Model 1 *betas* | Model 2 *betas* |
|---|---|---|
| **Profitability (Dependent)** | | |
| Riskiness | -0.1672 | -.1358 |
| Proactivness | -0.1577 | 0.0015 |
| Aggressiveness | | -.373** |
| Analysis | | -.425 |
| Defensiveness | | -.489*** |
| Futurity | | -.466*** |
| $R^2$ | 0.0145 | 0.1285 |
| $F$ | 0.619 | 1.966*** |
| Change $R^2$ | | 0.1097** |
| Change $F$ | | 1.089 |

N=88; *$p<.01$; **$p<.05$; ***$p<.10$

**Table 4.11**  (*cont.*)

**Test of Hypothesis Three: Part Four**
**The Link Between Strategic Orientation and Performance**

| Variables | Model 1 *betas* | Model 2 *betas* |
|---|---|---|
| **Employees for 1993 (Dependent)** | | |
| Riskiness | 11.99 | 13.866 |
| Proactivness | -35.29 | -53.69*** |
| Aggressiveness | | 23.799 |
| Analysis | | 32.61 |
| Defensiveness | | 6.37 |
| Futurity | | 28.66 |
| $R^2$ | 0.0188 | 0.0641 |
| $F$ | 0.804 | 0.913 |
| Change $R^2$ | | 0.0453 |
| Change $F$ | | 0.109 |

N=88; *$p<.01$; **$p<.05$; ***$p<.10$

**Test of Hypothesis Three: Part Five**
**The Link Between Strategic Orientation and Performance**

| Variables | Model 1 *betas* | Model 2 *betas* |
|---|---|---|
| **Sales Growth Per Employee (Dependent)** | | |
| Riskiness | 1.58 | -1.84 |
| Proactivness | 18.92 | 33.25 |
| Aggressiveness | | -8.22 |
| Analysis | | -11.56 |
| Defensiveness | | -22.05 |
| Futurity | | -40.35 |
| $R^2$ | 0.0124 | 0.072 |
| $F$ | 0.526 | 1.034 |
| Change $R^2$ | | 0.0596 |
| Change $F$ | | 0.508 |

N=88; *$p<.01$; **$p<.05$; ***$p<.10$

**Table 4.11 (cont.)**

**Test of Hypothesis Three: Part Six**
**The Link Between Strategic Orientation and Performance**

| Variables | Model 1 *betas* | Model 2 *betas* |
|---|---|---|
| **Employee Growth (Dependent)** | | |
| Riskiness | 13.58 | 11.86 |
| Proactivness | -28.32 | -39.29 |
| Aggressiveness | | 23.21 |
| Analysis | | 25.70 |
| Defensiveness | | 6.31 |
| Futurity | | 17.67 |
| $R^2$ | 0.0175 | 0.0573 |
| $F$ | 0.747 | 0.811 |
| Change $R^2$ | | 0.0398 |
| Change $F$ | | 0.064 |

N=88; $*p<.01$; $**p<.05$; $***p<.10$

The results on Hypothesis Three were mixed. Although there was some significance among the models, there was little ability to explain large amounts of the variance in the performance of new ventures with strategic orientation. The support for this hypothesis was weaker than expected.

Specifically, the findings demonstrated a positive link between riskiness and sales growth. Interestingly the same model contained a negative relationship between proactivness and sales growth. The same type of finding was also true of new venture revenues. Riskiness was found to have a positive relationship to new venture revenues and proactivness was found to have a negative relationship to new venture revenues. Riskiness appeared to increase the growth of new ventures and proactivness appeared to decrease the growth of new ventures. The only other significant regression was the full model with profitability as the dependent variable. Aggressiveness, defensiveness, and futurity all show a weak negative relationship with profitability. None of the other regressions were significant. Clearly, there was some support for a link between strategic orientation and new venture performance but the level of variance explained was quite low.

## THE LINK BETWEEN ENVIRONMENT AND PERFORMANCE

The fourth hypothesis proposes a link between the environment and the performance of new ventures. Because there is no theoretical priority for the environmental variables, traditional regressions are conducted on these indicators. Table 4.12 shows the outcomes of these analyses.

As can be seen from Table 4.12 little empirical support existed for a link between environment and new venture performance. The only significant link was a negative relationship between dynamic environments and sales in the most recent year reported. Beyond this small amount of explained variance, little evidence existed in this study to support Hypothesis Four. Therefore there was limited support for Hypothesis Four.

**Table 4.12  Regressions Testing the Link Between Environment and Performance**

| Dependents: | Growth | Sales93 | Profit | Employ93 | Salgrper | Employ Growth |
|---|---|---|---|---|---|---|
| Independents | *betas* | *betas* | *betas* | *betas* | *betas* | *betas* |
| Dynamism | -267.83 | -9540.9* | 0.034 | -27.85 | 17.73 | -23.86 |
| Competitive Threat | -256.36 | -1801.9 | 0.113 | -1.50 | 1.35 | 4.40 |
| Complexity | -128.62 | 2779.1 | -.225 | 6.65 | -7.84 | 9.04 |
| $R^2$ | 0.028 | 0.1065 | 0.0395 | 0.033 | 0.028 | 0.035 |
| F | *0.788* | *3.297**1.138* | | *0.929* | *0.807* | *0.989* |

N=88; *$p$<.01; **$p$<.05; ***$p$<.10

## LINKING THE INTERACTION OF STRATEGY AND ENVIRONMENT TO PERFORMANCE

Hypothesis five, the final hypothesis in this study explores what has traditionally been found to be the most important explanatory variable (McDougall, 1987), the interaction between strategy and environment. Hierarchial regression was the analytic strategy used with these variables. The hierarchy was based on the strategic orientation variables of riskiness and proactivness. Table 4.13 presents the findings related to Hypothesis Five. Since only the results of the regressions linking the interaction of strategic orientation and dynamism were significant, only those results were presented in this chapter. The results of the interactions between competitive threat-strategic orientation and complexity-strategic orientation are presented in Appendix J.

**Table 4.13  Test of Hypothesis Five: The Link Between the Strategic Orientation-Dynamism Interaction and New Venture Performance**

| Variables | Model 1 *betas* | Model 2 *betas* |
|---|---|---|
| **Sales Growth (Dependent)** | | |
| Risk x Dynamism | -517.27 | -954.19*** |
| Proactivness x Dynamism | 578.52 | 1166.85** |
| Aggressiveness x Dynamism | | 46.65 |
| Analysis x Dynamism | | -173.56 |
| Defensiveness x Dynamism | | 573.02 |
| Futurity x Dynamism | | -674.94 |
| $R^2$ | 0.0464 | 0.1311 |
| $F$ | 2.041 | 2.12*** |
| Change $R^2$ | | 0.0847 |
| Change $F$ | | 0.079 |

N=88; *$p<.01$; **$p<.05$; ***$p<.10$

**Table 4.13  (*cont.*)**

**Test of Hypothesis Five: The Link Between the Strategic Orientation-Dynamism Interaction and New Venture Performance**

| Variables | Model 1 *betas* | Model 2 *betas* |
|---|---|---|
| **Sales In 1993 (Dependent)** | | |
| Risk x Dynamism | -12957* | -21586* |
| Proactivness x Dynamism | 13795* | 21519* |
| Aggressiveness x Dynamism | | 1627 |
| Analysis x Dynamism | | 18.94 |
| Defensiveness x Dynamism | | 10103** |
| Futurity x Dynamism | | -11897** |
| $R^2$ | 0.21 | 0.36 |
| $F$ | 10.85* | 7.42* |
| Change $R^2$ | | 0.15* |
| Change $F$ | | -3.43 |

N=88; *$p<.01$; **$p<.05$; ***$p<.10$

**Test of Hypothesis Five: The Link Between the Strategic Orientation-Dynamism Interaction and New Venture Performance**

| Variables | Model 1 *betas* | Model 2 *betas* |
|---|---|---|
| **Profit as a Range (Dependent)** | | |
| Risk x Dynamism | 0.11 | 0.54 |
| Proactivness x Dynamism | -.13 | -.04 |
| Aggressiveness x Dynamism | | -.28 |
| Analysis x Dynamism | | -.19 |
| Defensiveness x Dynamism | | -.13 |
| Futurity x Dynamism | | 0.07 |
| $R^2$ | 0.043 | 0.063 |
| $F$ | 0.183 | 0.89 |
| Change $R^2$ | | 0.02 |
| Change $F$ | | 0.71 |

N=88; *$p<.01$; **$p<.05$; ***$p<.10$

**Table 4.13** (*cont.*)

**Test of Hypothesis Five: The Link Between the Strategic Orientation-Dynamism Interaction and New Venture Performance**

| Variables | Model 1 *betas* | Model 2 *betas* |
|---|---|---|
| **1993 # of Employees (Dependent)** | | |
| Risk x Dynamism | -31.53*** | -15.52 |
| Proactivness x Dynamism | 32.12 | 49.05 |
| Aggressiveness x Dynamism | | 14.98 |
| Analysis x Dynamism | | 35.42 |
| Defensiveness x Dynamism | | -29.52 |
| Futurity x Dynamism | | -48.76 |
| $R^2$ | 0.0548 | 0.092 |
| $F$ | 2.436*** | 1.35 |
| Change $R^2$ | | 0.0372 |
| Change $F$ | | 1.086 |

N=88; *$p<.01$; **$p<.05$; ***$p<.10$

**Test of Hypothesis Five: The Link Between the Strategic Orientation-Dynamism Interaction and New Venture Performance**

| Variables | Model 1 *betas* | Model 2 *betas* |
|---|---|---|
| **Sales Growth Per Employee (Dependent)** | | |
| Risk x Dynamism | 18.60 | 22.89 |
| Proactivness x Dynamism | -23.35 | -44.20 |
| Aggressiveness x Dynamism | | -8.38 |
| Analysis x Dynamism | | 3.56 |
| Defensiveness x Dynamism | | 3.11 |
| Futurity x Dynamism | | 18.96 |
| $R^2$ | 0.024 | 0.0468 |
| $F$ | 1.005 | 0.654 |
| Change $R^2$ | | 0.023 |
| Change $F$ | | 0.351 |

N=88; *$p<.01$; **$p<.05$; ***$p<.10$

**Table 4.13** (*cont.*)

**Test of Hypothesis Five: The Link Between the Strategic Orientation-Dynamism Interaction and New Venture Performance**

| Variables | Model 1 *betas* | Model 2 *betas* |
|---|---|---|
| **Employee Growth (Dependent)** | | |
| Risk x Dynamism | -28.63*** | -11.79 |
| Proactivness x Dynamism | 29.12 | 39.16 |
| Aggressiveness x Dynamism | | 11.74 |
| Analysis x Dynamism | | 38.26 |
| Defensiveness x Dynamism | | -26.66 |
| Futurity x Dynamism | | -44.82 |
| $R^2$ | 0.0824 | 0.104 |
| $F$ | 2.797*** | 1.542 |
| Change $R^2$ | | 0.022 |
| Change $F$ | | -1.255 |

N=88; *$p<.01$; **$p<.05$; ***$p<.10$

The link between the strategy-environment interaction was supported by the findings in Table 4.13. The interaction of dynamism and strategic orientation explain about 35 percent of the variation in new venture revenues. The number of employees and employee growth were also significant. One should note that, in all three cases, risky actions and proactive actions in dynamic environments had similar effects on different performance measures. Simply, proactive actions in dynamic environments appeared to improve performance and risky strategic actions in dynamic environments appeared to inhibit performance. The level of competitive threat appeared to have no effect on new venture performance. The complexity-strategy interaction did not have its proposed effect either. However, a link appeared to exist between the interaction of strategy and dynamic environments and firm performance for entrepreneurial firms. Therefore Hypothesis Five was partially supported.

## TEST OF THE FULL MODEL

This section is devoted to a discussion of the results of a full model hierarchial regression. The full model is a regression model with all of the variables of the theoretical model included. The hierarchial order was: skill heterogeneity, educational demography, conflict, strategy, environment, and the strategy-environment interactions. This order was exactly as proposed in the theoretical model. Table 4.14 presents the results of the full model for new venture revenues. The four of the other five hierarchial regressions were not significant and all five were presented in Appendix K. Table 4.14 follows the reporting of these results.

The six stage hierarchial regression with new venture growth as the dependent variable explained a total of 49 percent of the variation. However was quite low from a parsimony standpoint. The first stage in the growth model included skill heterogeneity and team size. These two variables had an adjusted $r$-square of 16 percent. The adjusted $r$-square on model six containing 34 variables was still only 16 percent. The important variable in this series of regressions was team size. However, the strategy variables riskiness and proactivness and heterogeneity of degree were also significant in models four and five.

The full model explains about 65 percent of the total variation in new venture revenues. The adjusted *r-square* for new venture revenues was .46. In fact the adjusted $r$-squared changed only minutely between model one and model six. The important positive variables in the significant third level of the full model were heterogeneity of major in highest degree and the strategic orientation variables aggressiveness and riskiness. Heterogeneity of major in highest degree was negatively associated with revenues and the strategy variables were positively associated with revenues. The findings on the strategy variables were supported by previous research (Miller and Camp, 1985; Miller, 1983). In the full new venture revenues model, the skill heterogeneity variable, degree, aggressiveness, and the interaction of dynamism and proactivness and riskiness were significant.

Notice that the interactions were the most powerful force affecting the significance of the model. Cohen and Cohen (1983) note that these variables would be interactions and not moderators because the three variables used to create the interaction variables were significant without the interaction variables in the model and non-significant when those variables were included.

Overall, some support for all the hypotheses except the first one exists. There does seem to be a link between conflict and strategic orien-

**Table 4.14  Full Model Test**
**Six Stage Hierarchical Regression**

| Dependent Variables | Model 1 | Model 2 | Model 3 | Model 4 | Model 5 | Model 6 |
|---|---|---|---|---|---|---|
| **1993 Sales** | | | | | | |
| **Variables** | | | | | | |
| Skill Heterogeneity | 1230.93 | 658.07 | 699.22 | -126.35 | 3335.78 | 9170** |
| Team Size | 3325.06 | 7485.60 | 7679.33 | 8395.14 | 5939.59 | 6044 |
| Degree | | 450.81 | 2490.94 | -5479.09 | -1972.53 | -2741 |
| Major | | -30742.90** | -30188.48** | -42303.40* | -42519.43* | -31762** |
| Function | | -21956.41*** | -23533.76*** | -9973.97 | -10377.66 | -8990 |
| Cognitive Conflict | | | -2297.13 | -2038.67 | -1192.50 | -2416 |
| Affective Conflict | | | 1038.823 | 421.62 | 179.61 | 639 |
| Aggressiveness | | | | 7294.31** | 5438.30 | 7007** |
| Analysis | | | | 10624.58 | 10918.17 | 1392 |
| Defensiveness | | | | -5855.42 | -4444.10 | -2502 |
| Futurity | | | | 1398.74 | 334.02 | -2794 |
| Proactivness | | | | -9539.18 | -10594.39*** | 7683 |
| Riskiness | | | | 12963.60** | 11975.78** | -9485 |
| Competitive Threat | | | | | -593.20 | -5682 |
| Complexity | | | | | 3273.59 | -25398 |
| Dynamism | | | | | -8757.80** | 60005 |
| Competitive x Aggressiveness | | | | | | -1699 |

| Dependent | Model 1 | Model 2 | Model 3 | Model 4 | Model 5 | Model 6 |
|---|---|---|---|---|---|---|
| Competitive x Analysis | | | | | | -11381 |
| Competitive x Defensiveness | | | | | | 3878 |
| Competitive x Futurity | | | | | | 1894 |
| Competitive x Proactivness | | | | | | 5996 |
| Competitive x Riskiness | | | | | | 491 |
| Complexity x Aggressiveness | | | | | | 2933 |
| Complexity x Analysis | | | | | | 11784 |
| Complexity x Defensiveness | | | | | | 1626 |
| Complexity x Futurity | | | | | | -8828 |
| Complexity x Proactivness | | | | | | 699 |
| Complexity x Riskiness | | | | | | 2450 |
| Dynamism x Aggressiveness | | | | | | -1982 |
| Dynamism x Analysis | | | | | | -18046 |
| Dynamism x Defensiveness | | | | | | 5803 |
| Dynamism x Futurity | | | | | | 172 |
| Dynamism x Proactivness | | | | | | 29496* |
| Dynamism x Riskiness | | | | | | -36763* |
| $R^2$ | 0.0052 | 0.1054 | 0.1208 | 0.2643 | 0.3368 | 0.6541 |
| *F* | 0.22 | 1.93*** | 1.57 | 2.04** | 2.25* | 2.95* |
| Change $R^2$ | | 0.1002* | 0.0154 | 0.1435* | 0.073*** | 0.32** |
| Change *F* | | -1.71 | -0.36 | 0.47 | 0.21 | 0.7 |

N=88; *p<.01; **p<.05; ***p<.10

tation. A link between strategic orientation and performance also seems to exist. A link also exists between the environment and performance and the interaction of strategy-environment and performance. The next chapter clarifies these findings. What do they mean? Chapter Five shows where this study fits with previous studies and the value of this research from a theoretical and an empirical perspective.

# CHAPTER 5

# Conclusions and Implications

The purpose of this final chapter is to discuss the findings of this study in the context of current theory and practice. This chapter brings the findings of this study into focus in the context of previous studies of new venture performance and clarifies this study's historical significance. This chapter presents the additions to the paradigms of entrepreneurship and strategic management made by this study.

This chapter is arranged in three major sections. The first section describes the historical significance of this study and contains conclusions about the entrepreneurial team extension to the new venture performance model. The second major section describes the extension of the new venture performance model to include a more complete conception of the environment and its interaction with strategic orientation. The argument in the second section being that the environmental scheme conceptualized improves the understanding of the influence of organizational task environment on new venture performance. A summary of the strategic orientation-performance link conclusions follows these two major sections. This chapter is concluded by a section which contains three short discussions; one section discuses the limitations of this study and another presents the practical implications. The final section outlines specific future research and challenges entrepreneurship researchers to expand their views of organizational models.

## THE HISTORICAL CONTEXT OF THE RESEARCH: GAINING PERSPECTIVE FROM PAST AND PRESENT EMPIRICAL FINDINGS

This study builds on a stream of research which has its recent history with Sandberg's (1986) dissertation (see Appendix A for a list of new venture performance studies). The most recent study which parallels Sandberg's work is Robinson's (1995) dissertation which is a replication of McDougall's dissertation. The current study, however, is deemed a departure from previous studies in two ways. First, an attempt is made, as suggested by Gartner, Shaver, Gatewood, and Katz (1994) and Herron (1990), to put the entrepreneur back into the model. There is sufficient theoretical support for the inclusion of the "ET" in the new venture performance model. There are some intriguing findings from the empirical results of this study which support the inclusion of the entrepreneurial team in the new venture performance model. Findings presented in Chapter Four lend support to the idea that entrepreneurial team affective and cognitive conflict are linked to new venture strategic orientation. Empirical connections are then made between strategic orientation and new venture performance. Stronger empirical links exist between the strategy-environment interaction and new venture performance.

The creation of this fit between industry environment and strategy is the job of the entrepreneurial team. It is the entrepreneurial team that understands the environment and the strategies of the firm well enough to make them fit and meld. This study derived evidence to support such a notion. Specifically, risky strategies appear to be a much more logical choice for new ventures in stable environments. Further, new ventures in unstable environments should choose strategies that preempt the actions of their competitors. In this study affective and cognitive conflict influence the firm's ability make strategy and environment fit. The choice of strategy was influenced by the conflict levels of the entrepreneurial team and therefore effects the fit between strategy and environment. It is clear that the entrepreneurial team is an important predictor of new venture performance what ever the nature of that relationship.

There is also evidence of a direct link between entrepreneurial teams and new venture performance. Skill heterogeneity is significant in the final model when the model is more fully specified and therefore when statistical inference is far more reliable. Heterogeneity of major in highest degree has a negative effect on new venture performance. Simply put, individual differences between team members tend to have negative effects on new venture performance.

There were also indicators of entrepreneurial team effects on new venture growth. As with Siegal, Siegal, and MacMillian (1993), the size of the entrepreneurial team influences the rate of firm growth. It is not clear, however, whether it is firm growth that causes the need for the team or if it is the team that causes the firm to grow. Given that team size has no effect on any of the other measures of new venture performance it could be that the growth of the firm necessitates the existence of the team. However, it is difficult to build a causal argument without further replication.

Taken together these findings support the inclusion of the entrepreneurial team in the new venture performance model. The behaviors, attitudes, composition, and size of the entrepreneurial team indirectly and directly affect the performance of the new venture. Skill heterogeneity, heterogeneity of major in highest degree, and team size have direct effects on the performance of the firm. Affective and cognitive conflict have indirect effects on new venture performance. Understanding these variables and their effect on new venture performance could lead to double digit improvement in performance.

The inclusion of some form of the entrepreneurial team in the new venture performance model is both logical and probable. Sandberg (1986) notes that his small study of eight firms is not sufficient evidence to delete the entrepreneur from the model. In the same vein, this study's larger sample does not contain sufficient evidence that the entrepreneurial team should always be included in the new venture performance model. Further study of expanded models with reliable and valid scales are necessary before a more complete and scientific view of the new venture performance can be established.

Most of the recent new venture performance research dismissed Sandberg's (1986) arguments about the role of the entrepreneur in new venture performance. Since Sandberg's research, the major new venture studies have simply not included any form of the entrepreneur as a part of their theoretical model (Kunkel, 1991; McDougall, 1987; Robinson, 1995). Sandberg (1986) vehemently argued in the last chapter of his book that the entrepreneur or "E" should be left in the new venture performance model. The major new venture studies since Sandberg's assumed that entrepreneurs did not have any influence on new venture performance. This study clearly demonstrates that such an assumption may have been far to restrictive. Gartner (1985; 1988) suggests that the entrepreneur is often mis-specified as a construct in empirical research. This study certainly supports his assertion. This study shows clearly that when reliable and valid scales are used, and a sufficient theoretical frame is established, that new venture performance models that include some form of the entrepreneur explain greater amounts of variation in new venture performance. In this study the entrepreneur is reconfigured to the entrepreneurial team, with dramatically different results from past studies. The next section describes the expanded conceptualization of industry environment and the possible performance effects of a new venture's industry environment.

## THE SECOND EXPANSION OF THE NEW VENTURE PERFORMANCE MODEL: CONCEPTUALIZING THE INFLUENCE OF THE ENVIRONMENT ON NEW VENTURE PERFORMANCE

The second extension of the entrepreneurship paradigm in this study comes from the standpoint of conceptualization and measurement of the industry environment. This study used Aldrich's (1979) conception and Dess and Beard's (1984) theoretical and empirical refinement of the environment. The researcher attempted to avoid the environmental measurement surrogates which have come under methodological attack (Dess, Hitt, and Ireland, 1990; Snyder and Glueck, 1982; Tosi, Aldag, and Storey, 1973). The criticisms of the surrogate measures of the environment are cast on two bases. First, the surrogates exhibit a large amount of measurement error. Second, they give little detail as to the nature of industry dynamics. Most often they are some measure built around the level of competition or they are simply the perceptions of industry environment that chief executives use to make decisions (Duncan, 1972). Recent studies are replete with qualitative examples of firms that succumb to environmental forces other than competition as measured by industry structure (Miller, 1993, 1990; Mintzberg, 1987, 1994). Measures of the environment must go beyond industry structure or even industry concentration to be effective. The findings of this study are helpful in understanding the details of the role of the industry environment and the strategy-environment interactions. Firms in this study were effected by the environment on only a limited basis. However, dynamism had an effect on the performance of the firm itself and the strategies that the firm could logically pursue and continue to perform well. Findings about industry structure and its link to firm performance are far less informative or generalizable. It should not be surprising that new ventures in an oligopoly show above average returns but how does environmental instability affect a firm's rate of return? How does competitive threat affect new venture growth and revenues? In this study, dynamism is much more powerful than the level of industry competition or the complexity of the industry. Environmental change which has been cited for years as a powerful force on large firms (Mintzberg, 1973) in particular because of their inability to avoid the forces of the environment also effects new ventures. The power of the environment for these firms is not in environmental competitiveness or environmental complexity but in the speed and magnitude of environmental change.

In this study dynamism interacted with strategic orientation to explain far more variance than any of the other variables in the model. Evidence from this sample indicates that risky actions in volatile environments lead to lower performance. However, risky actions in stable organizational task environments lead to higher performance. The main environmental contingency with this group of entrepreneurial firms is unpredictable environmental change. Proactive strategies lead to lower revenues in stable environments, but in dynamic environments, proactive strategies increase revenues. Simply, proactive actions such as market penatration tend to lower revenues overall, but in a highly dynamic environments, where change is constant and unpredictable such proactive strategies improve new venture performance. The firms that pursue these proactive strategies are attempting to nullify the effect of the environmental change. Risky strategies in hostile environments, however, have the opposite effect because they raise risk to illogical levels. Therefore, emerging firms should lead the industry in highly dynamic industry environments with proactive strategies.

## Summary of Environmental Conclusions

In previous new venture performance studies, the variables with the highest variance explained have been the strategy-environment interaction variables (Kunkel, 1991; McDougall et al., 1992; Robinson, 1995). Evidence of an interaction effect is also supported in this study. To explain the proactivness findings, one can draw from Miller's (1993) simplicity research. Miller argued that preemptive actions keep firms from failure by breaking single-loop learning traps. These preemptive strategic actions in dynamic environments improve new venture performance by changing the firm's approach before it becomes stale (Miller and Friesen, 1984; Staw et al., 1981).

Riskiness would appear to be a two edge sword. First, risky actions in general appear to increase revenues. However, it would appear that taking risky actions in an unstable industry environments has strong negative effects on new venture revenues. An explanation for these findings could perhaps be found on the dark side of entrepreneurship. Carland and Carland (1993) explained that sometimes entrepreneurs take highly risky actions with undaunted surety. Entrepreneurs often act as if the risk is not real or does not exist (Brockhaus, 1980). However research such as Keats and Hitt (1988) suggests that significant chance for loss of resources and market share exists in highly dynamic environments. Dean and Meyer (1996) also found that entrepreneurial firms often lack the resources necessary to address changes in volatile environments. Dean and Meyer argued that resources give entrepreneurial firms the ability to react to changes in the external environment and therefore improve performance. Interestingly, Sharfman and Dean (1991) who originated the particular form of organizational task environment measures used here found that Dynamism had the greatest negative influence on overall industry performance. It could be that the findings about Dynamism were generalizable to all types of firms.

In this case, the direct effect of change is not so much the issue as is the state of strategy and the ability of the firm to change strategy once changes have occurred in the industry environment. Previous the research has found that this particular group of firms was highly focused (Ensley and Banks, 1992). Miller (1993) would argue that they are extraordinarily good at one particular strategy. The question is what happens when the industry environment or opportunity window is destroyed? What happens when the fit that existed before the environmental change occurred no longer exists? In the case of this particular group of firms, they must be carefully proactive. The next section contains a short discussion of this study's conclusions about the strategic orientation performance link in new ventures.

## CONCLUSIONS ABOUT THE STRATEGY-PERFORMANCE LINK

The idea that strategy is one of the major determinants of new venture performance is not new. However, the approach in this study is a bit different than the main stream new venture studies of the past decade. Researchers in the fairly distant past considered strategy an important construct in the new venture performance model even before Sandberg's (1986) study, but few studies before Sandberg's empirically or conceptually clarified the strategy construct and its role in new venture performance (Biggadike, 1976 and Hobson and Morrision, 1983). Studies that followed Sandberg (1986) further clarified the role of strategy in new venture performance from a more situational standpoint (McDougall et al., 1992; Kunkel, 1991; Robinson, 1995). However, few studies did what Ginsberg (1984) warned was necessary to avoid high levels of measurement error, validate and check the reliability of the scales or measurements of strategy. An effort was made in this study to reduce measurement error and to clarify the role of certain strategic characteristics in new venture performance.

In this study the dimensions of strategic orientation were all posed to have a positive relationship to new venture performance. It however is not surprising that the relationships were not all positive and therefore contrary to current research (Lumpkin and Dess, 1996).

The findings in Chapter Four represent a mixed picture of the strategy performance relationship. Certainly a relationship exists but often the strategic orientation of the new venture had a negative relationship to new venture revenues, growth, and profitability. Proactivness for instance, had a negative relationship to new venture growth and revenues. This could be because of the cost of such activities and the reduced focus on what had been working. However, in a dynamic environment proactivness yielded positive performance. Riskiness had just the opposite effect on new venture performance. It appeared to enhance performance by itself, but when interacting with the environment, it reduced performance. So the strategy is important but the match of strategy and industry environment is far more important.

The other strategic dimensions ranged from no influence on new venture performance at all to only a mild effect on new venture profitability or revenues. Aggressiveness had a negative effect on profitability but a positive effect on revenues. Defensiveness and futurity had negative effects on new venture profitability. Analysis had no relationship to any of the new venture performance variables. Variance explained for all of the significant regressions was less than 20 percent. The most important variables were Miller's (1983) original entrepreneurial strategic orientation variables: riskiness and proactiveness.

Strategy was an important determinant of new venture performance in this and previous new venture studies and should be included in future studies. What should be clear for future studies was the importance of reliable and valid scales. Future efforts should improve the measurement of strategy and specifically focus on the characteristics of strategy which have the influence new venture performance.

## THE FULL MODEL

The hierarchial regression in Table 4.14 shows consistent findings across the analysis. The entrepreneurial team, strategic orientation, environment, and the strategy-environment interaction were all important variables in the new venture performance model. This full hierarchial regression analysis supports a great deal of the model presented in Appendix B. The change in *r-square* was significant in four of the six steps in the hierarchial regression. In the end, 65 percent (adjusted *r-square* of 46 percent) of the variation in new venture revenues could be attributed to the variables in the full model. Riskiness, proactivness, and dynamism were non-significant in Model Six confirming the existence of the strategy-environment interaction effect (Cohen and Cohen, 1983).

## THE PRACTICAL IMPLICATIONS OF THIS STUDY

Several practical implications were derived from this study. Several of these implications surround the development of the entrepreneurial team. As with other types of teams, the finding that cognitive conflict raises the level of affective conflict is important. Amason (1996) argued that it takes an exceptional team to increase cognitive conflict without raising the level of affective conflict. In addition, as with Amason's study, affective conflict had detrimental effects on the choice of strategic orientation in this sample. Therefore, work must ensue on the part of entrepreneurial team leaders to manage the level of conflict in their teams. Additionally, entrepreneurial team skill diversity should be high. Skill heterogeneity had a direct positive link to new venture performance.

From a strategic perspective, dynamic environments probably offer the greatest opportunity for loss and gain. Opportunities seem to open up in those environments, but danger lurks for those who are not aware of the environmental instability. Entrepreneurs should be aware of the environment, do environmental assessment often, and constantly conceptualize the environment. Finally, the practitioner should not stray from taking preemptive competitive actions. Although the action could lower short term performance, a preemptive action in a changing environment could produce strong positive revenue growth.

## LIMITATIONS OF THIS STUDY

This section describes the limitations of this study. The *inc. 500* firms grow at an average growth rate far in excess of the average new venture.

It could be that the relationships among team level variables, organizational level variables, and the environment are different for extremely high growth firms.

The method provides few limitations. In general, The scales were reliable and valid beyond a couple of low reliability coefficients. Venkatraman (1989) and Ginsberg (1984) were clear that the continuing development of scales was necessary for the field of strategic management to progress. Although refinement of the scales used in this study would certainly improve their value, there was little evidence that these scales did not function as intended. Non-response bias which is often a concern with survey research, was also not apparent. Nor were the assumptions of regression analysis violated. Clearly though, there are limitations to survey research and survey data. Ginsberg (1984) argued that survey data offered an avenue for generalizability, but survey data tends to lack the full breadth of complex constructs such as strategy. Common method variance which is often cited as a major problem with this type of organizational research is also less of a problem with this study because measures of internal, external, and performance variables all came from different sources.

## SUGGESTIONS FOR FUTURE RESEARCH

Suggestions for future research start with one of the variables in the expanded new venture performance model: the entrepreneurial team. The entrepreneurial team has both a direct and indirect influence on new venture performance. Future studies should fully explore the processes of the entrepreneurial team in an effort to understand its full influence on new venture performance. For the purposes of expanding the number and quality of suggested future teams research, Gladstein's (1984) group process model is used as a guide to additional group constructs which might be included in future new venture performance studies.

In future studies additional group composition variables should be included. Organizational and job tenure, industry experience, team experience, group demography, and other individual heterogeneity variables should be explored. Group structure variables such as role and goal clarity, work norms, task control, and formal group leadership structure should be examined for links to new venture performance. There is a wealth of research which has explored these constructs and the fields of social psychology, sociology, organizational behavior, and strategic management can all add both theoretically and methodologically to these efforts. The resources available to the group such as creativity, capital, expertise, and market potential should also be evaluated. The resource based view in strategic management could be especially helpful in this effort. Some of this research has developed logical measurement schemes which should be adopted and adapted by entrepreneurship researchers. Group cohesion, a common construct in group studies, should also be explored by new venture researchers.

This study justifies a much deeper and stronger look at the entrepreneurial team. How is strategy discussed within the entrepreneurial team? What is the role of consensus in entrepreneurial teams and what is the effect of consensus on new venture performance? Additionally, the complexity of the tasks of the entrepreneurial team and the level of environmental uncertainty should be examined for possible new venture performance effects. How does the compensation of entrepreneurial team member influence team level variables and therefore firm performance?

Future studies should also use the expanded measures of the industry environment to find links between environment and new venture performance. Environmental profiles might be valuable. Are there industries which are entrepreneurship-friendly? Do the *inc.* 500 and the *Fortune* 500 occupy different core industries? Are environmental characteristics different among emerging and established firms? These questions would go a long way in explaining the role of the environment in the both established and emerging firms.

Additional effort should also be made to further clarify the strategic orientation variables. For instance, innovativeness, which was not a part of the STROBE scale, has been suggested by Miller and Friesen (1983) and Lumpkin and Dess (1996) to be an important entrepreneurial strategic orientation variable and should be included in future new venture performance studies. Ginsberg (1984) suggested over a decade ago that the development of reliable and valid measures of strategy was an important aspect of paradigm development. To date little has been done beyond Venkatraman's STROBE scale.

This study was partially developed to suggest that the field of entrepreneurship break the mold of the traditional new venture performance study, employ logical theoretical development, and expand the new venture performance model beyond the traditional three variables. Gartner (1985) suggested a decade ago, that the new venture process is complex and difficult to model with a parsimonious set of variables. If that is the case, then the field has arbitrarily reduced the number of variables in the new venture performance model. Future research should increase the number of logically derived new venture performance indicators, and the entrepreneurial team and entrepreneurial team behaviourial or attitudinal variables are a good source of variables for this expansion.

When researching and working with entrepreneurs, researchers need to catch some of the spirit that they hold. Entrepreneurship is a diverse discipline with roots in almost every field. However, the new venture performance model has been dominated by ideas of only one or two fields and really only one or two schools of thought. There are probably hundreds of variables that affect the performance of new ventures and a fully specified model will probably never be developed, but it is worth a try. The economic development benefits could be endless.

# Constructs Included in New Venture Performance Models

**Table A.1. Constructs Included in New Venture Performance Models**

| Study | Sample | NVP Model Constructs |
|---|---|---|
| Biggadike (1976) | 68 PIMS start-ups | Entrepreneur and Strategy |
| Von Hippel (1977) | 21 Fortune 100 Ventures | Entrepreneur and Capitalization |
| Hobson and Morrision (1983) | 117 PIMS start-ups | Entrepreneur and Strategy |
| Sandberg (1986) | 17 ventures supported from venture capital firms | Entrepreneur, Strategy, and Industry Structure |
| Miller and Camp (1985) | 84 PIMS adolescents | Strategy |
| MacMillian and Day (1987) | 81 PIMS start-ups | Strategy |
| Romanelli (1987) | 108 minicomputer start-ups | Strategy and Industry Stage |
| McDougall (1987) | 247 high technology ventures | Strategy, Origin, Industry Structure, and Interactions |
| Stuart and Abetti (1987) | 52 high technology ventures | Environment, Strategy, Structure, and Entrepreneur |

**Table A.1.** (*cont.*)

| Study | Sample | NVP Model Constructs |
|-------|--------|----------------------|
| Hall (1989) | 4 venture capitalists | Subjective Judgment |
| Kunkel (1991) | 82 growth oriented ventures | Strategy, Industry Structure, and the Interaction |
| McCarthy (1992) | 2994 NFIB members | Strategy, Environment, Resources, and Change |
| Bolland (1993) | 101 high technology ventures | Origin, Strategy, and Industry Structure |
| Blunden (1993) | 41 ventures supported by venture capital firms | Capitalization and Type of Funding |
| Jenssen (1991) | 148 Norwegian ventures | Entrepreneur and Industry |
| Stearns et al. (1995) | 1900 new ventures | Location, Strategy, Industry, and Interactions |

Adapted from McDougall et al. (1992).

# A Model of the Impact of Entrepreneurial Team Skill Heterogeneity and Affective and Cognitive Conflict on the Strategic Orientation and Performance of New Ventures

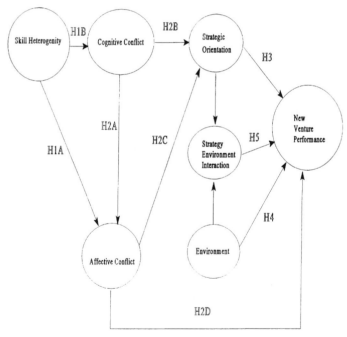

**Figure B.1. A Model of the Impact of Entrepreneurial Team Skill Heterogeneity and Affective and Cognitive Conflict on the Strategic Orientation and Performance of New Ventures**

# Commonly Measured Empirical Dimensions of Strategic Orientation

**Table C.1. Commonly Measured Empirical Dimensions of Strategic Orientation**

| Author(s) | Dimensions Measured | Use/Purpose |
|---|---|---|
| Miller and Friesen (1982) | Innovativeness, Riskiness Proactiveness, Analysis, Futurity | Measure Strategic Posture* |
| Miller (1993) | Innovativeness, Riskiness, Proactiveness | Measure Correlates of Entrepreneurial Strategies |
| Miller and Friesen (1983) | Riskiness, Proactiveness, Analysis, Futurity, Innovativeness | Measure Strategic Orientation |
| Miller (1988) | Differentiation, Innovation | Measure Strategic Orientation |
| Venkatraman (1989) | Riskiness, Proactiveness, Analysis, Futurity, Aggresiveness, Defensiveness | Measure Strategic Orientation |
| Covin and Slevin (1989) | Riskiness, Proactiveness, Innovativeness | Measure Strategic Orientation |
| Covin (1991) | Riskiness, Proactiveness, Innovativeness | Measure Strategic Orientation |

**Table C.1.** (*cont.*)

| Author(s) | Dimensions Measured | Use/Purpose |
|---|---|---|
| Naman and Slevin (1993) | Riskiness, Proactiveness, Innovativeness | Entrepreneurial Style |
| Tan and Litschert (1994) | Analysis, Defensiveness, Futurity, Riskiness, Proactiveness | Measure Strategic Orientation |
| Merz and Sauber (1995) | Proactivness, Innovativeness, Riskiness | Measure Strategic Orientation |

*Remember for the purposes of this study strategic orientation, strategic posture, and business level strategy are considered the same dimension. All of the above studies with the exception of Venkatraman (1989) utilized these dimensions of strategy in an effort to measure strategies on a dimension between entrepreneurialism and conservatism.

# Empirically Validated Environmental Dimensions

**Table D.1. Empirically Validated Environmental Dimensions**

| One Dimension | Two Dimensions | Three Dimensions |
|---|---|---|
| Bourgeois (1985) | Duncan (1972) | Miller (1987) |
| Volatility (P/O) | Complexity (P) | Dynamism (P) |
| | Dynamism | Heterogeneity |
| Snyder and Glueck (1982) | | Hostility |
| Volatility (P/O) | Miller and Friesen (1983) | |
| | Dynamism (P) | Dess and Beard (1984) |
| Fredrickson (1984) | Heterogeneity | Munificence (O) |
| Stability (O) | | Dynamism |
| | Naman and Slevin (1993) | Complexity |
| Fredrickson and Mitchell | Hostility (P) | |
| (1984) | Dynamism | Keats and Hitt (1988) |
| Stability (O) | | Munificence (O) |
| | | Dynamism |
| Tosi, Aldag, and Storey | | Complexity |
| (1973) | | |
| Volatility (O) | | Lawless and Finich |
| | | (1989) |
| Covin and Slevin (1989) | | Dynamism (O) |
| Hostility (P) | | Complexity |
| | | Munificence |

**Table D.1.** (*cont.*)

| One Dimension | Two Dimensions | Three Dimensions |
|---|---|---|
| | | Sharfman and Dean (1991) |
| | | Competitive Threat (O) |
| | | Dynamism |
| | | Complexity |
| | | |
| | | McArthur and Nystrom (1991) |
| | | Munificence (O) |
| | | Dynamism |
| | | Complexity |

P = Perceptual; O = Objective (Adapted and updated from Dess, Ireland, and Hitt (1990))

# Survey Instrument and Cover Letters

Survey Instrument and Cover Letters
Understanding Entrepreneurial Team Dynamics

The following questions attempt to discover how the dynamics of teams of entrepreneurs impact the strategic posture and financial performance of entrepreneurial firms. By answering and returning the questionnaire you will contribute greatly to the understanding of how such firms operate.

Responses for questions 1-9 are:      1=A Great Deal
                                       2=Quite a Bit
                                       3=A Moderate Amount
                                     4=Very Little
                                     5=None

1. How much emotional conflict is there among the members of your entrepreneurial team......................1   2   3   4   5

2. How much anger is there generally among the members of your entrepreneurial team in discussions concerning strategic decisions...........................................................1   2   3   4   5

3. How much personal friction is there among entrepreneurial team members concerning strategic decisions........1   2   3   4   5

4. How much are personality clashes between team members evident during discussions of strategic decisions......1   2   3   4   5

5. How much tension is there generally in the entrepreneurial group during discussions of strategic decisions.......1   2   3   4   5

6. How much disagreement is there generally among the members of the entrepreneurial team over their opinions concerning strategic decisions.......................................................1   2   3   4   5

7. How many disagreements over different ideas about strategic decisions are there generally...................1   2   3   4   5

8. How many differences about the content of strategic decisions does the entrepreneurial team generally have......1   2   3   4   5

9. How many differences of opinion are there within the top management group during the discussion of strategic decisions........................................................1   2   3   4   5

Responses for questions 10-16 are:      **NE**=Not Effective
                                         **SE**=Seldom Effective
                                       **ME**=Moderately Effective
                                       **LE**=Largely Effective
                                       **EE**=Extremely Effective

10. My skill in the detailed design of our products/services is:..............................................NE  SE  ME  LE  EE

11. My skill in evaluating the various functions of our organization:.........................................NE  SE  ME  LE  EE

12. My skill in understanding our industry and the implications of it trends and changes is:.....................NE  SE  ME  LE  EE

13. My skill in motivating and influencing the behavior of our employees is: ..................................NE  SE  ME  LE  EE

14. My skill in creating relations with and influencing important people outside our organization is:..............NE  SE  ME  LE  EE

15. My skill in planning and administering our business' activities is........................................NE  SE  ME  LE  EE

16. My skill in discovering opportunities to profitably change our business is:...............................NE  SE  ME  LE  EE

Responses for questions 17-45 are:

**SA**=Strongly Agree
**A**=Agree
**N**=No Opinion
**D**=Disagree
**SD**=Strongly Disagree

17. This firm tends to sacrifice profitability to gain market share. . . . . . . . . . . . . . . . . . . . . . . . . . . . . . . . . . . . . . . . . . . .SA  A  N  D  SD

18. This firm tends to cut prices to gain market share. . . . . . . . . . . . . . . . . . . . . . . . . . . . . . . . . . . . . . . . . . . . . . . .SA  A  N  D  SD

19. This firm tends to set prices below the competition. . . . . . . . . . . . . . . . . . . . . . . . . . . . . . . . . . . . . . . . . . . . . . SA  A  N  D  SD

20. This firm tends to seek market share position at the expense of cash flow and profitability. . . . . . . . . . . . . . . . . . . . . . SA  A  N  D  SD

21. This firm emphasizes effective coordination among different functional areas. . . . . . . . . . . . . . . . . . . . . . . . . . . . . . SA  A  N  D  SD

22. Information systems provide support for decision making. . . . . . . . . . . . . . . . . . . . . . . . . . . . . . . . . . . . . . . . . . . .SA  A  N  D  SD

23. When confronted with a major decision, this firm usually try to develop solutions through analysis. . . . . . . . . . . . . . SA .A  N  D  SD

24. This firm uses planning techniques. . . . . . . . . . . . . . . . . . . . . . . . . . . . . . . . . . . . . . . . . . . . . . . . . . . . . . . . . . . .SA  A  N  D  SD

25. This firm uses the outputs of management information and control systems. . . . . . . . . . . . . . . . . . . . . . . . . . . . . . .SA  A  N  D  SD

26. This firm uses manpower planning and performance appraisal of senior managers. . . . . . . . . . . . . . . . . . . . . . . . . . .SA  A  N  D  SD

27 This firm has engaged in significant modifications to its manufacturing technology. . . . . . . . . . . . . . . . . . . . . . . . . .SA  A  N  D  SD

28. This firm uses cost control systems for monitoring performance. . . . . . . . . . . . . . . . . . . . . . . . . . . . . . . . . . . . . . . .SA  A  N  D  SD

29. This firm uses production management techniques. . . . . . . . . . . . . . . . . . . . . . . . . . . . . . . . . . . . . . . . . . . . . . . . . .SA  A  N  D  SD

30. This firm emphasizes product quality through the use of total quality management. . . . . . . . . . . . . . . . . . . . . . . . . . SA  A  N  D  SD

31. Our criteria for resource allocation generally reflects short-term consideration. . . . . . . . . . . . . . . . . . . . . . . . . . . . SA  A  N  D  SD

32. We emphasize basic research to provide us with a future competitive edge. . . . . . . . . . . . . . . . . . . . . . . . . . . . . . .SA  A  N  D  SD

33. This firm forecasts key indicators of operations. . . . . . . . . . . . . . . . . . . . . . . . . . . . . . . . . . . . . . . . . . . . . . . . . . . SA  A  N  D  SD

34. This firm formally tracks significant general trends. . . . . . . . . . . . . . . . . . . . . . . . . . . . . . . . . . . . . . . . . . . . . . . . SA  A  N  D  SD

35. This firm uses "what-if" analysis on critical issues. . . . . . . . . . . . . . . . . . . . . . . . . . . . . . . . . . . . . . . . . . . . . . . . SA  A  N  D  SD

36. This firm constantly seeks new opportunities related to present operations. . . . . . . . . . . . . . . . . . . . . . . . . . . . . . . SA  A  N  D  SD

37. This firm is usually the first ones to introduce new brands or products in the market. . . . . . . . . . . . . . . . . . . . . . . . .SA  A  N  D  SD

38. This firm is constantly on the look out for businesses that can be acquired. . . . . . . . . . . . . . . . . . . . . . . . . . . . . . . . SA  A  N  D  SD

39. Competitors generally preempt this firm expanding capacity before this firm does . . . . . . . . . . . . . . . . . . . . . . . . . . SA  A  N  D  SD

40. Operations in later/larger stages of the product life cycle are strategically eliminated. . . . . . . . . . . . . . . . . . . . . . . SA  A  N  D  SD

41. This firm's operations can be generally characterized as high-risk. . . . . . . . . . . . . . . . . . . . . . . . . . . . . . . . . . . . . . . . . . . . . . .SA A N D SD

42. This firm seems to adopt a rather conservative view when making major decisions. . . . . . . . . . . . . . . . . . . . . . . . . . . .SA A N D SD

43. New products are approved on a "stage-by-stage" basis rather than with "blanket" approval. . . . . . . . . . . . . . . . . . . .SA A N D SD

44. This firm has a tendency to support projects where the expected returns are certain. . . . . . . . . . . . . . . . . . . . . . . . . . .SA A N D SD

45. Operations of this firm have generally followed the "tried and true" paths. . . . . . . . . . . . . . . . . . . . . . . . . . . . . . . . . . .SA A N D SD

46. How often are new strategic plans developed by this firm? _____

47. How many people founded this firm? ____

48. How many of the founders remain active in this firm's day-to-day operations? _____

49. Are you a founder of this firm?
    Yes ____          No ____

50. Do you own 10% or more of this firm?
    Yes ____          No ____

51. Do you consider yourself an entrepreneur?
    Yes ____          No ____

52. Have you previously owned a business?
    Yes ____          No ____          If yes how many? _____

53. Is this firm owned by more than one person?
    Yes ____          No ____

54. Is this firm a publicly traded corporation?
    Yes ____          No ____

55. What is your gender?
    Male ____      Female ____

56. What is your highest degree? (circle one)

                    High School   Associate   Bachelors   Masters   Doctorate

57. What was your major for your highest degree? _____

58. What is the functional area of your current position? (Circle One)

Legal   Accounting   General Business   Marketing   Engineering   Research & Development   Production/Operations   Miscellaneous

If there is anything further you wish to tell us about entrepreneurial teams or the development of strategy in entrepreneurial firms, please feel free to do so on the back of this page. Any comments you have will help us understand the strategy process in entrepreneurial firms.

Thank you for your participation. It is truly appreciated!!!!
Please return this questionnaire to:  Michael D. Ensley (PH: (501) 450-3149)
                         Department of Management and Marketing, College of Business Administration
                         The University of Central Arkansas, Conway  Arkansas  72035

DATE

FIELD(name)
FIELD(inc name)
FIELD(address)
FIELD(city)

The development and growth of new ventures is critical to the economic well-being of the United States. For this to happen on more than a "hit or miss" basis, we need to understand more about the process. One prominent entrepreneur in the athletic footwear industry once told me that he never planned. Another prominent entrepreneur in the computer industry told me he could not survive without his plan. How critical is planning, especially strategic planning, to entrepreneurial firms? What role does it play in their success? These are among many questions this research hopes to answer. I hope you will volunteer a few minutes of your valuable time to complete the enclosed questionnaire.

Your firm is among the nation's fastest growing and most entrepreneurial. For this reason information about your use of strategic planning would be of great value and interest to many people around the country and abroad. Because your firm is one of only one hundred firms selected from the entire country to represent all entrepreneurial firms it is important that your questionnaire be completed and returned.

You may be assured that your individual responses will remain confidential. The questionnaire has an identification number, but this is **FOR MAILING PURPOSES ONLY.** It will allow us to check your name off of the mailing list when your questionnaire is returned and therefore save further mailing costs.

The combined results of all the questionnaires will be made available, through articles in journals, to both entrepreneurs and those interested in new venture growth and development. You may receive a summary of results by writing "copy of results requested" on the back of the return envelope, and printing your name and address below it. **Please do not put this information on the questionnaire itself.**

I will be happy to answer any questions you might have. Please write or call. The telephone number is (501) 450-3149.

Thank you for your assistance.

Sincerely,


Michael D. Ensley

**Letter for Second Mailing**

DATE

FIELD(Name1)
FIELD(Company name)
FIELD(address)

About six weeks ago I wrote seeking your opinion on the importance and state of strategy and strategic planning among entrepreneurial teams. As of today I have not yet received your completed questionnaire.

The large number of questionnaires returned is very encouraging. But, your individual response is important so that I can describe the phenomenon of the entrepreneurial team, its choice of strategy, and the interactions of the team members. **YOUR** individual response is important. You have perspectives on strategy, planning, and the entrepreneurial team that no one else has. It is important that you respond today.

The development and growth of new ventures is critical to the economic well-being of the United States. For this to happen on more than a "hit or miss" basis, we need to understand more about the process. One prominent entrepreneur in the athletic footwear industry once told me that he never planned. Another prominent entrepreneur in the computer industry told me he could not survive without his plan. How critical is planning, especially strategic planning, to entrepreneurial firms? What role does it play in their success? These are among many questions this research hopes to answer. I hope you will volunteer a few minutes of your valuable time to complete the enclosed questionnaire.

Your firm is among the nation's fastest growing and most entrepreneurial. For this reason information about your use of strategic planning would be of great value and interest to many people around the country and abroad. Because your firm is one of only about one hundred firms selected from the entire country to represent all entrepreneurial firms it is important that your questionnaire be completed and returned.

You may be assured that your individual responses will remain completely confidential. Your responses will be seen by no one but me and my support staff. The questionnaire has an identification number, but this is **FOR MAILING PURPOSES ONLY.** It will allow us to check your name off of the mailing list when your questionnaire is returned and therefore save further mailing costs.

The combined results of all the questionnaires will be made available, through articles in journals, to both entrepreneurs and those interested in new venture growth and development. You may receive a summary of results by writing "copy of results requested" on the back of the return envelope, and printing your name and address below it. **Please do not put this information on the questionnaire itself.**

I will be happy to answer any questions you might have. Please write or call. The telephone number is (501) 450-5306.

Thank you for your assistance.

Sincerely,


Michael D. Ensley
Assistant Professor of Strategic Management and Entrepreneurship

# Definition and Calculation of the Environmental Dimensions

**Table F.1. Definition and Calculation of the Dynamism Dimension**

| Indicator | Calculation | Data Source |
|---|---|---|
| 1. Dynamism Measure | | |
| 1.A Market Instability (MI) | Standard error of the regression slope of industry revenues over 1985-1994 divided by the mean of market revenues | All of the commerce oriented census, and all of the annual surveys produced from 1982 to the present, U.S. Bureau of the Census. |
| 1.B Number of Employees Instability (NEI) | Same procedure as 1.A using the total number of employees. | 1982-1994 County Business Patterns, U.S. Bureau of the Census. 1994-1995 Hours, Wages, and Earnings, Bureau of Labor Statistics. |
| 1.C Technological Instability (TI) | Same procedure as 1.A using research and development intensity. | Compustat Database |
| Dynamism Measure (DM) | $DM = Z(MI+NEI) + Z(TI) +10*$ | |

Adapted from Sharfman and Dean (1991).

**Table F.2. Definition and Calculation of the Competitive Threat Dimension**

| Indicator | Calculation | Data Source |
|---|---|---|
| 2. Competitive Threat | | |
| 2.A Revenues Munificence (RM) | Regression slope of industry revenues over 1985-1994 divided by the mean values of shipments. | Same as 1.A |
| 2.B Number of Employees Munificence (NEM) | Same procedure as 2.A using the total number of employees. | Same as 1.A |
| 2.C Number of Firms in the Eight Firm Concentration Ratio (NF) | Total number of different firms appearing in the top eight market share holders in the data sets from 1990, 1993, and 1996. | Ward's Business Directory, Volume five for the years 1990, 1993, and 1996. |
| 2.D. Average Market Share Change (MSC) | Each firm that appeared in both 1990 and 1996 was selected for analysis. Each firm's market share was compared across the time periods and the absolute value of the change was calculated. The average of these absolute values was then used as average market share change. | Same as 2.C. |
| Competitive Threat Measure (CT) | $CT=Z(\sqrt{NF\times MSC})/$ $(10.05+MUN)$ | Where MUN=RM+NEM |

**Table F.3. Definition and Calculation of the Complexity Dimension**

| Indicator | Calculation | Data Source |
|---|---|---|
| 3. Complexity Measure | | |
| 3.A Geographic Concentration of Firms (GCNF) | Sum of the total number of firms in a census division squared divided by the total number of firms in that census division quantity squared. | 1994 County Business Patterns, U.S. Bureau of Census. |
| 3.B Geographic Concentration of the Number of Employees (GCNE) | Same procedure as 3.A using total number of employees. | Same as 3.A |
| 3.C. Percentage of Scientists and Engineers (SE) | Estimated employee levels of all scientists and engineers as a percentage of the total workforce in an industry. | Bureau of Labor Statistics WWW site under Gopher@special requests |
| 3.D Number of eight Digit (product level) SIC codes (SDC) | Total number of product categories in each industry. | Dun and Bradstreet's industrial classification manual. |
| Complexity Measure (CM) | $CM=Z(EPC) + Z(TC) - Z(GC) + 10$ | |

\* Z scores were used to insure that all scale values were on the same metric.
\* The various linear transformations that have been used were done to prevent the calculation from creating meaningless numbers. It was assumed that an environmental dimension could only be non-existent and not negative. Therefore the limits of all three dimensions are 0 and positive infinity.

# Summary Table of Scale Items and Measures

**Table G.1. Summary Table of Scale Items and Measures**

| Construct | Source | # of Items | # of Dimensions |
|---|---|---|---|
| Skill Heterogeneity | Herron (1990) | Seven | One |
| Conflict | Amason and Harrison (1995) | Nine | Two |
| Strategic Orientation | Venkatraman (1989) | Twenty-nine | Six |
| Environment | Sharfman and Dean (1991) | Eleven | Three |

APPENDIX H

# Results of Tests of Hypothesis Five: The Link Between the Strategic Orientation-Environmental Interaction and New Venture Performance

**Table H.1. Test of Hypothesis Five**
**The Link Between the Strategic Orientation-Complexity**
**Interaction and New Venture Growth**

| Variables | Model 1 *betas* | Model 2 *betas* |
|---|---|---|
| **Sales Growth (Dependent)** | | |
| Risk x Complexity | -514.27 | -435.53 |
| Proactiveness x Complexity | 607.01 | 922.32 |
| Aggressiveness x Complexity | | 73.51 |
| Analysis x Complexity | | 173.04 |
| Defensiveness x Complexity | | -95.24 |
| Futurity x Complexity | | -528.41 |
| $R^2$ | 0.0207 | 0.0325 |
| $F$ | 0.886 | 0.447 |
| Change $R^2$ | | -0.0118 |
| Change $F$ | | -.439 |

N=88; *$p<.01$; **$p<.05$; ***$p<.10$

**Table H.2. Test of Hypothesis Five**
**The Link Between the Strategic Orientation-Complexity**
**Interaction and New Venture Revenues**

| Variables | Model 1 *betas* | Model 2 *betas* |
|---|---|---|
| **Sales In 1993 (Dependent)** | | |
| Risk x Complexity | 1510 | -744 |
| Proactiveness x Complexity | -2212 | -1722 |
| Aggressiveness x Complexity | | 609 |
| Analysis x Complexity | | -5956 |
| Defensiveness x Complexity | | 1637 |
| Futurity x Complexity | | 4487 |
| $R^2$ | 0.0019 | 0.0133 |
| $F$ | 0.078 | 0.179 |
| Change $R^2$ | | -0.0114 |
| Change $F$ | | -0.101 |

N=88; $*p<.01$; $**p<.05$; $***p<.10$

**Table H.3. Test of Hypothesis Five**
**The Link Between the Strategic Orientation-Complexity**
**Interaction and New Venture Profitability**

| Variables | Model 1 *betas* | Model 2 *betas* |
|---|---|---|
| **Profit (Dependent)** | | |
| Risk x Complexity | 0.09 | 0.09 |
| Proactiveness x Complexity | -0.16 | -0.30 |
| Aggressiveness x Complexity | | 0.07 |
| Analysis x Complexity | | 0.13 |
| Defensiveness x Complexity | | -0.11 |
| Futurity x Complexity | | 0.09 |
| $R^2$ | 0.0087 | 0.0195 |
| $F$ | 0.370 | 0.265 |
| Change $R^2$ | | -0.0108 |
| Change $F$ | | -0.105 |

N=88; $*p<.01$; $**p<.05$; $***p<.10$

**Table H.4. Test of Hypothesis Five**
**The Link Between the Strategic Orientation-Complexity**
**Interaction and New Venture Employment**

| Variables | Model 1 *betas* | Model 2 *betas* |
|---|---|---|
| **Employ93 (Dependent)** | | |
| Risk x Complexity | 10.81 | 9.12 |
| Proactiveness x Complexity | -15.04 | 6.66 |
| Aggressiveness x Complexity | | 2.34 |
| Analysis x Complexity | | -42.80 |
| Defensiveness x Complexity | | 0.87 |
| Futurity x Complexity | | 14.23 |
| $R^2$ | 0 .0029 | 0.0284 |
| $F$ | 0.123 | 0.390 |
| Change $R^2$ | | -0.0255 |
| Change $F$ | | -0.267 |

N=88; *$p<.01$; **$p<.05$; ***$p<.10$

**Table H.5. Test of Hypothesis Five**
**The Link Between the Strategic Orientation-Complexity**
**Interaction and New Venture Sales Per Employee**

| Variables | Model 1 *betas* | Model 2 *betas* |
|---|---|---|
| **Sales Growth per Employee (Dependent)** | | |
| Risk x Complexity | 20.62 | 15.20 |
| Proactiveness x Complexity | -28.41 | -75.60 |
| Aggressiveness x Complexity | | . 0.04 |
| Analysis x Complexity | | 17.81 |
| Defensiveness x Complexity | | -4.44 |
| Futurity x Complexity | | 43.40 |
| $R^2$ | 0.0198 | 0.1162 |
| $F$ | 0.849 | 1.753 |
| Change $R^2$ | | -0.0964 |
| Change $F$ | | -0.904 |

N=88; *$p<.01$; **$p<.05$; ***$p<.10$

**Table H.6. Test of Hypothesis Five**
**The Link Between the Strategic Orientation-Complexity**
**Interaction and New Venture Employee Growth**

| Variables | Model 1 *betas* | Model 2 *betas* |
|---|---|---|
| **Employee Growth (Dependent)** | | |
| Risk x Complexity | 8.62 | 6.76 |
| Proactiveness x Complexity | -11.42 | 3.68 |
| Aggressiveness x Complexity | | 2.39 |
| Analysis x Complexity | | -33.48 |
| Defensiveness x Complexity | | 0.11 |
| Futurity x Complexity | | 13.67 |
| $R^2$ | 0.0021 | 0.0229 |
| $F$ | 0.088 | 0.312 |
| Change $R^2$ | | -0.0208 |
| Change $F$ | | -0.224 |

N=88; *$p<.01$; **$p<.05$; ***$p<.10$

**Table H.7. Test of Hypothesis Five**
**The Link Between the Strategic Orientation-Competitive Threat**
**and New Venture Growth**

| Variables | Model 1 *betas* | Model 2 *betas* |
|---|---|---|
| **Sales Growth (Dependent)** | | |
| Risk x Competitive Threat | -128.72 | -129.04 |
| Proactiveness x Cometitive Threat | 58.32 | 785.26 |
| Aggressiveness x Competitive Threat | | 60.43 |
| Analysis x Competitive Threat | | -578.20 |
| Defensiveness x Competitive Threat | | 87.62 |
| Futurity x Competitive Threat | | -392.62 |
| $R^2$ | 0.0164 | 0.0831 |
| $F$ | 0.700 | 1.208 |
| Change $R^2$ | | -0.0667 |
| Change $F$ | | -0.508 |

N=88; *$p<.01$; **$p<.05$; ***$p<.10$

**Table H.8. Test of Hypothesis Five**
**The Link Between the Strategic Orientation-Competitive Threat Interaction and New Venture Revenues**

| Variables | Model 1 *betas* | Model 2 *betas* |
|---|---|---|
| **Sales 1993 (Dependent)** | | |
| Risk x Competitive Threat | 685 | -5384.92 |
| Proactiveness x Competitive Threat | -2676.38 | -2519.78 |
| Aggressiveness x Competitive Threat | | 1712.82 |
| Analysis x Competitive Threat | | -5623.39 |
| Defensiveness x Competitive Threat | | 4648.72 |
| Futurity x Competitive Threat | | 3899.91 |
| $R^2$ | 0.0336 | 0.0683 |
| $F$ | 1.459 | 0.977 |
| Change $R^2$ | | -0.0347 |
| Change $F$ | | -0.482 |

N=88; *$p$<.01; **$p$<.05; ***$p$<.10

**Table H.9. Test of Hypothesis Five**
**The Link Between the Strategic Orientation-Competitive Threat Interaction and New Venture Profitability**

| Variables | Model 1 *betas* | Model 2 *betas* |
|---|---|---|
| **Profit (Dependent)** | | |
| Risk x Competitive Threat | 0.16 | 0.17 |
| Proactiveness x Competitive Threat | -0.15 | -0.18 |
| Aggressiveness x Competitive Threat | | 0.05 |
| Analysis x Competitive Threat | | 0.30 |
| Defensiveness x Competitve Threat | | -0.06 |
| Futurity x Competitive Threat | | -0.22 |
| $R^2$ | 0.017 | 0.0333 |
| $F$ | 0.728 | 0.460 |
| Change $R^2$ | | -0.0163 |
| Change $F$ | | -0.268 |

N=88; *$p$<.01; **$p$<.05; ***$p$<.10

**Table H.10. Test of Hypothesis Five**
**The Link Between the Strategic Orientation-Competitive Threat**
**Interaction and New Venture Employment**

| Variables | Model 1 *betas* | Model 2 *betas* |
|---|---|---|
| **Employ93 (Dependent)** | | |
| Risk x Competitive Threat | 38.75 | -0.39 |
| Proactiveness x Competitive Threat | -46.34 | -66.79 |
| Aggressiveness x Competitive Threat | | 21.05 |
| Analysis x Competitive Threat | | -11.92 |
| Defensiveness x Competitive Threat | | 14.64 |
| Futurity x Competitive Threat | | 31.30 |
| $R^2$ | 0.0434 | 0.0939 |
| $F$ | 1.905 | 1.381 |
| Change $R^2$ | | -0.0505 |
| Change $F$ | | -0.524 |

N=88; *$p$<.01; **$p$<.05; ***$p$<.10

**Table H.11. Test of Hypothesis Five**
**The Link Between the Strategic Orientation-Competitive Threat**
**Interaction and New Venture Sales Growth Per Employee**

| Variables | Model 1 *betas* | Model 2 *betas* |
|---|---|---|
| **Sales Growth per Employee (Dependent)** | | |
| Risk x Competitive Threat | 3.36 | 1.45 |
| Proactiveness x Competitive Threat | -4.12 | -11.47 |
| Aggressiveness x Competitive Threat | | 2.22 |
| Analysis x Competitive Threat | | 6.45 |
| Defensiveness x Competitive Threat | | -2.16 |
| Futurity x Competitive Threat | | 3.94 |
| $R^2$ | 0.0006 | 0.0032 |
| $F$ | 0.03 | 0.04 |
| Change $R^2$ | | -0.0026 |
| Change $F$ | | -0.01 |

N=88; *$p$<.01; **$p$<.05; ***$p$<.10

**Table H.12. Test of Hypothesis Five**
**The Link Between the Strategic Orientation-Competitive Threat**
**Interaction and New Venture Employee Growth**

| Variables | Model 1 *betas* | Model 2 *betas* |
|---|---|---|
| **Employee Growth (Dependent)** | | |
| Risk x Competitive Threat | 28.10 | 3.42 |
| Proactiveness x Competitive Threat | -34.66 | -53.54 |
| Aggressiveness x Competitive Threat | | 18.24 |
| Analysis x Competitive Threat | | -8.41 |
| Defensiveness x Competitive Threat | | 9.92 |
| Futurity x Competitive Threat | | 21.08 |
| $R^2$ | 0.0316 | 0.0872 |
| $F$ | 1.39 | 1.274 |
| Change $R^2$ | | -0.0556 |
| Change $F$ | | -0.116 |

N=88; *p<.01; **p<.05; ***p<.10

# Tests of the Full Model

**Table I.1. Full Model Test**
**Six Stage Hierarchical Regression**

| Dependent | Model 1 | Model 2 | Model 3 | Model 4 | Model 5 | Model 6 |
|---|---|---|---|---|---|---|
| **Number of Employees in 1993** | | | | | | |
| **Variables** | | | | | | |
| Skill Heterogeneity | -0.26 | -0.52 | -2.32 | -8.77 | -0.02 | 7.07 |
| Team Size | 30.63 | 26.04 | 27.03 | 29.48 | 21.06 | 24.20 |
| Degree | | 64.88 | 78.95 | 54.17 | 62.73 | 102.19 |
| Major | | -91.43 | -92.37 | -102.07 | -103.65 | -73.71 |
| Function | | 81.20 | 72.43 | 99.27 | 97.58 | -24.56 |
| Cognitive Conflict | | | -13.36 | -16.00 | -14.19 | -37.03* |
| Affective Conflict | | | 10.00 | 8.77 | 8.50 | 16.83 |
| Aggressiveness | | | | 36.30 | 31.28 | 41.57 |
| Analysis | | | | 32.77 | 35.40 | -5.66 |
| Defensiveness | | | | 6.54 | 11.25 | -3.03 |
| Futurity | | | | 29.68 | 27.34 | 40.77 |
| Proactiveness | | | | -37.94 | -40.47 | 18.31 |
| Riskiness | | | | 15.33 | 11.86 | -46.00 |
| Competitive Threat | | | | | -.46 | 5.50 |
| Complexity | | | | | 4.99 | -416.44 |
| Dynamism | | | | | -25.85 | 186.88 |
| Competitive x Aggressiveness | | | | | | 56.11 |
| Competitive x Analysis | | | | | | -82.28 |

| Dependent | Model 1 | Model 2 | Model 3 | Model 4 | Model 5 | Model 6 |
|---|---|---|---|---|---|---|
| Competitive x Defensiveness | | | | | | -23.73 |
| Competitive x Futurity | | | | | | 17.96 |
| Competitive x Proactiveness | | | | | | -25.64 |
| Competitive x Riskiness | | | | | | 21.19 |
| Complexity x Aggressiveness | | | | | | 37.78 |
| Complexity x Analysis | | | | | | 46.59 |
| Complexity x Defensiveness | | | | | | 24.64 |
| Complexity x Futurity | | | | | | 36.06 |
| Complexity x Proactiveness | | | | | | -24.78 |
| Complexity x Riskiness | | | | | | 23.94 |
| Dynamism x Aggressiveness | | | | | | 13.09 |
| Dynamism x Analysis | | | | | | -3.93 |
| Dynamism x Defensiveness | | | | | | -51.37 |
| Dynamism x Futurity | | | | | | -15.24 |
| Dynamism x Proactiveness | | | | | | 16.40 |
| Dynamism x Riskiness | | | | | | -25.79 |
| $R^2$ | 0.0135 | 0.0486 | 0.0722 | 0.1413 | 0.1636 | 0.3785 |
| F | 0.58 | 0.84 | 0.89 | 0.94 | 0.87 | 0.95 |
| Change $R^2$ | | -0.0351 | -0.0236 | -0.0691 | -0.0223 | -0.2149 |
| Change F | | -0.26 | -0.05 | -0.05 | 0.07 | -0.08 |

N=88; *p<.01; **p<.05; ***p<.10

**Table I.2. Full Model Test**
**Six Stage Hierarchical Regression**

| Dependent | Model 1 | Model 2 | Model 3 | Model 4 | Model 5 | Model 6 |
|---|---|---|---|---|---|---|
| **Sales Growth per Employee** | | | | | | |
| **Variables** | | | | | | |
| Skill Heterogeneity | 9.73 | 10.41 | 12.33 | 15.36 | 13.01 | 21.73 |
| Team Size | -8.22 | -11.41 | -11.29 | -9.25 | 2.14 | -3.69 |
| Degree | | -18.92 | -21.03 | -6.89 | -8.33 | 21.33 |
| Major | | 61.79 | 65.71 | 55.18 | 59.63 | 85.59 |
| Function | | -2.87 | -3.23 | -1.54 | 4.92 | -19.24 |
| Cognitive Conflict | | | -0.03 | 1.09 | 2.09 | 0.57 |
| Affective Conflict | | | -3.74 | -4.70 | -6.16 | -6.56 |
| Aggressiveness | | | | -7.13 | -4.49 | -20.68 |
| Analysis | | | | -16.84 | -25.22 | -1.45 |
| Defensiveness | | | | -24.19 | -29.96 | -29.58 |
| Futurity | | | | -41.29 | -42.16 | -93.96* |
| Proactiveness | | | | 28.13 | 27.81 | 79.50** |
| Riskiness | | | | -6.91 | -1.85 | -17.90 |
| Competitive Threat | | | | | -3.42 | 94.76 |
| Complexity | | | | | 12.86 | 101.10 |
| Dynamism | | | | | 21.84 | -257.05 |
| Competitive x Aggressiveness | | | | | | -7.53 |
| Competitive x Analysis | | | | | | -47.18 |

| Dependent | Model 1 | Model 2 | Model 3 | Model 4 | Model 5 | Model 6 |
|---|---|---|---|---|---|---|
| Competitive x Defensiveness | | | | | | 5.41 |
| Competitive x Futurity | | | | | | -8.61 |
| Competitive x Proactiveness | | | | | | 7.90 |
| Competitive x Riskiness | | | | | | 4.01 |
| Complexity x Aggressiveness | | | | | | -1.82 |
| Complexity x Analysis | | | | | | -7.79 |
| Complexity x Defensiveness | | | | | | 13.60 |
| Complexity x Futurity | | | | | | 8.67 |
| Complexity x Proactiveness | | | | | | -15.03 |
| Complexity x Riskiness | | | | | | -32.47 |
| Dynamism x Aggressiveness | | | | | | -15.23 |
| Dynamism x Analysis | | | | | | 117.97** |
| Dynamism x Defensiveness | | | | | | 45.79 |
| Dynamism x Futurity | | | | | | -65.84 |
| Dynamism x Proactiveness | | | | | | -0.58 |
| Dynamism x Riskiness | | | | | | 31.65 |
| $R^2$ | 0.0057 | 0.0216 | 0.0338 | 0.1039 | 0.1462 | 0.2953 |
| F | 0.24 | 0.36 | 0.40 | 0.66 | 0.76 | 0.65 |
| Change $R^2$ | | -0.0159 | -0.0122 | -0.0701 | -0.0423 | -0.1491 |
| Change F | | -0.12 | -0.04 | -0.26 | -0.10 | 0.11 |

N=88; *p<.01; **p<.05; ***p<.10

**Table I.3. Full Model Test**
**Six Stage Hierarchical Regression**

| Dependent | Model 1 | Model 2 | Model 3 | Model 4 | Model 5 | Model 6 |
|---|---|---|---|---|---|---|
| **Employee Growth** | | | | | | |
| **Variables** | | | | | | |
| Skill Heterogeneity | -.89 | -1.06 | -3.00 | -9.14 | -3.65 | 6.13 |
| Team Size | 20.65 | 17.14 | 18.13 | 21.21 | 15.02 | 18.91 |
| Degree | | 48.13 | 62.35 | 45.53 | 47.70*** | 85.62 |
| Major | | -68.61 | -69.84 | -82.90 | -86.07 | -49.46 |
| Function | | 62.78 | 54.05 | 81.00 | 80.68 | -30.31 |
| Cognitive Conflict | | | -13.34 | -16.28 | -14.50 | -33.50* |
| Affective Conflict | | | 10.27 | 9.09 | 8.31 | 14.83 |
| Aggressiveness | | | | 34.84** | 30.86 | 38.25 |
| Analysis | | | | 25.52 | 28.73 | -1.07 |
| Defensiveness | | | | 7.26 | 12.21 | -3.71 |
| Futurity | | | | 20.34 | 18.73 | 26.74 |
| Proactiveness | | | | -24.60 | -29.35** | 16.87 |
| Riskiness | | | | 11.27 | 9.53** | -40.18 |
| Competitive Threat | | | | | 5.69 | -17.76 |
| Complexity | | | | | 6.79 | -337.14 |
| Dynamism | | | | | -20.98 | 154.37 |
| Competitive x Aggressiveness | | | | | | 52.46** |
| Competitive x Analysis | | | | | | -70.70 |

| Dependent | Model 1 | Model 2 | Model 3 | Model 4 | Model 5 | Model 6 |
|---|---|---|---|---|---|---|
| Competitive x Defensiveness | | | | | | -21.13 |
| Competitive x Futurity | | | | | | 37.48 |
| Competitive x Proactiveness | | | | | | -33.89 |
| Competitive x Riskiness | | | | | | 14.71 |
| Complexity x Aggressiveness | | | | | | 37.22 |
| Complexity x Analysis | | | | | | 31.49 |
| Complexity x Defensiveness | | | | | | 18.11 |
| Complexity x Futurity | | | | | | 39.33 |
| Complexity x Proactiveness | | | | | | -19.68 |
| Complexity x Riskiness | | | | | | 10.80 |
| Dynamism x Aggressiveness | | | | | | 8.93 |
| Dynamism x Analysis | | | | | | 7.14 |
| Dynamism x Defensiveness | | | | | | -45.31 |
| Dynamism x Futurity | | | | | | -12.00 |
| Dynamism x Proactiveness | | | | | | 10.50 |
| Dynamism x Riskiness | | | | | | -22.12 |
| $R^2$ | 0.0084 | 0.0360 | 0.0693 | 0.1394 | 0.1616 | 0.3673 |
| F | 0.36 | 0.61 | 0.85 | 0.92 | 0.86 | 0.90 |
| Change $R^2$ | | -0.0276 | -0.0333 | -0.0701 | -0.0222 | -0.2057 |
| Change F | | -0.25 | -0.24 | -0.07 | 0.06 | -0.04 |

N=88; *p<.01; **p<.05; ***p<.10

**Table I.4. Full Model Test**
**Six Stage Hierarchical Regression**

| Dependent | Model 1 | Model 2 | Model 3 | Model 4 | Model 5 | Model 6 |
|---|---|---|---|---|---|---|
| **Sales Growth** | | | | | | |
| **Variables** | | | | | | |
| Skill Heterogeneity | -365.82 | -374.76 | -380.43 | -334.51 | -301.06 | 105.76 |
| Team Size | 1730.39* | 1959.93* | 1969.57* | 1902.15* | 1890.45* | 1984.58* |
| Degree | | -1267.39 | -1152.05 | -1881.03*** | -1771.03*** | -1197.25 |
| Major | | -275.85 | -262.77 | -587.32 | -541.17 | 16.21 |
| Function | | -891.04 | -972.09 | -600.67 | -625.82 | -579.36 |
| Cognitive Conflict | | | -120.32 | -6.55 | -15.67 | -113.62 |
| Affective Conflict | | | 69.59 | 44.93 | 58.90 | 91.90 |
| Aggressiveness | | | | -185.03 | -184.34 | -385.87 |
| Analysis | | | | 753.78 | 727.21 | 661.60 |
| Defensiveness | | | | -451.27 | -480.99 | -71.81 |
| Futurity | | | | 306.05 | 300.80 | -205.94 |
| Proactiveness | | | | -1111.57** | -1044.61** | 171.95 |
| Riskiness | | | | 1032.50** | 1008.00** | 181.82 |
| Competitive Threat | | | | | -145.69 | 1074.86 |
| Complexity | | | | | -71.35 | 587.70 |
| Dynamism | | | | | 14.03 | -2335.63 |
| Competitive x Aggressiveness | | | | | | -48.02 |
| Competitive x Analysis | | | | | | -696.47 |

| Dependent | Model 1 | Model 2 | Model 3 | Model 4 | Model 5 | Model 6 |
|---|---|---|---|---|---|---|
| Competitive x Defensiveness | | | | | | -362.33 |
| Competitive x Futurity | | | | | | -392.95 |
| Competitive x Proactiveness | | | | | | 531.86 |
| Competitive x Riskiness | | | | | | 396.90 |
| Complexity x Aggressiveness | | | | | | -343.64 |
| Complexity x Analysis | | | | | | 337.09 |
| Complexity x Defensiveness | | | | | | 217.94 |
| Complexity x Futurity | | | | | | -189.23 |
| Complexity x Proactiveness | | | | | | 179.19 |
| Complexity x Riskiness | | | | | | -342.54 |
| Dynamism x Aggressiveness | | | | | | -60.13 |
| Dynamism x Analysis | | | | | | 748.15 |
| Dynamism x Defensiveness | | | | | | 930.80 |
| Dynamism x Futurity | | | | | | -699.87 |
| Dynamism x Proactiveness | | | | | | 1151.20 |
| Dynamism x Riskiness | | | | | | -993.72 |
| $R^2$ | 0.1769 | 0.2127 | 0.2193 | 0.3483 | 0.3524 | 0.4881 |
| F | 9.13* | 4.43* | 3.21* | 3.04* | 2.41* | 1.49*** |
| Change $R^2$ | | -0.0358 | -0.0066 | -0.1290* | -0.0041 | -0.1357 |
| Change F | | 4.70 | 1.22 | 0.17 | 0.63 | 0.92 |

N=88; *p<.01; **p<.05; ***p<.10

**Table I.5. Full Model Test**
**Six Stage Hierarchical Regression**

| Dependent | Model 1 | Model 2 | Model 3 | Model 4 | Model 5 | Model 6 |
|---|---|---|---|---|---|---|
| 1993 Profit | | | | | | |
| **Variables** | | | | | | |
| Skill Heterogeneity | -0.16 | -0.15 | -0.15 | -0.07 | -0.17 | -0.20 |
| Team Size | -0.21 | -0.21 | -0.21 | -0.20 | -0.26 | -0.39 |
| Degree | | 0.12 | 0.11 | 0.15 | -0.03 | -0.12 |
| Major | | -0.76 | -0.75 | -0.50 | -0.59 | -0.08 |
| Function | | 0.80 | 0.81 | 0.64 | 0.63 | 0.54 |
| Cognitive Conflict | | | 0.01 | 0.08 | 0.04 | 0.12 |
| Affective Conflict | | | -0.02 | -0.05 | -0.03 | -0.05 |
| Aggressiveness | | | | -0.37 | -0.34 | -0.45 |
| Analysis | | | | -0.35 | -0.23 | 0.32 |
| Defensiveness | | | | -0.49 | -0.43 | -0.28 |
| Futurity | | | | -0.51 | -0.46 | -0.86 |
| Proactiveness | | | | -0.03 | -0.05 | -0.10 |
| Riskiness | | | | -0.02 | -0.03 | 0.06 |
| Competitive Threat | | | | | 0.17 | 0.94 |
| Complexity | | | | | -0.22 | 5.10 |
| Dynamism | | | | | -0.01 | 0.80 |
| Competitive x Aggressiveness | | | | | | -0.11 |
| Competitive x Analysis | | | | | | 0.69 |

| Dependent | Model 1 | Model 2 | Model 3 | Model 4 | Model 5 | Model 6 |
|---|---|---|---|---|---|---|
| Competitive x Defensiveness | | | | | | -0.20 |
| Competitive x Futurity | | | | | | -0.76 |
| Competitive x Proactiveness | | | | | | 0.15 |
| Competitive x Riskiness | | | | | | 0.14 |
| Complexity x Aggressiveness | | | | | | 0.02 |
| Complexity x Analysis | | | | | | -0.64 |
| Complexity x Defensiveness | | | | | | -0.55 |
| Complexity x Futurity | | | | | | -0.43 |
| Complexity x Proactiveness | | | | | | -0.09 |
| Complexity x Riskiness | | | | | | -0.28 |
| Dynamism x Aggressiveness | | | | | | -0.52 |
| Dynamism x Analysis | | | | | | 0.18 |
| Dynamism x Defensiveness | | | | | | 0.04 |
| Dynamism x Futurity | | | | | | -0.48 |
| Dynamism x Proactiveness | | | | | | 0.25 |
| Dynamism x Riskiness | | | | | | 0.37 |
| $R^2$ | 0.0144 | 0.0410 | 0.0417 | 0.1496 | 0.1904 | 0.3315 |
| F | 0.62 | 0.70 | 0.50 | 1.00 | 1.04 | 0.77 |
| Change $R^2$ | | -0.0266 | -0.376 | -0.1079 | -0.0408 | -0.1411 |
| Change F | | -0.08 | -0.2 | -0.50 | -0.04 | 0.27 |

N=88; *p<.01; **p<.05; ***p<.10

# References

Achilles, C. M. 1992. *How do we go about "knowing" the culture of our school?* Paper presented at the Annual Meeting of the National Council of Professors of Educational Administration.

Aldrich, H. 1979. *Organizations and Environments.* Englewood Cliffs, NJ: Prentice-Hall.

Amason, A. 1993. *Decision quality and consensus: Examining a paradox in the relationship of top management teams and organizational performance.* Unpublished doctoral dissertation, University of South Carolina, Columbia.

Amason, A. 1996. Distinguishing the effects of functional and dysfunctional conflict on strategic decision making: Resolving a paradox for top management teams. *Academy of Management Journal*, 39 (1): 123-148.

Amason, A., & Harrison, A. W. 1994. *A multidimensional measure of conflict for strategic decision-making research.* Working paper, Mississippi State University, Starkville.

Amason, A., & Schweiger, D. M. 1994. Resolving the paradox of conflict, strategic decision Making and organizational performance. *International Journal of Conflict Management*, 5: 239-253.

Andrews, K. R. 1971. The concept of corporate strategy. Homewood, Ill.: Richard D. Irwin.

Bain, J. 1956. *Barriers to new competition, their character and consequences in manufacturing industries.* Cambridge, MA: Harvard University Press.

Bain, J., & Qualls, P. D. 1987. *Industrial organization: A treatise.* Greenwich, CN: JAI Press.

Bantel, K. A.,& Jackson, S. E. 1989. Top management and innovations in banking: Does the composition of the top team make a difference? *Strategic Management Journal*, 10: 107-124.

Belsley, D. A., Kuh, E., & Welsch, R. E. 1980. *Regression Diagnostics: Identifying Influential Data and Sources of Collinearity*. New York, NY: John Wiley & Sons.

Biggadike, R. C. 1976. *Corporate Diversification: Entry, Strategy, and Performance*. Cambridge, MA: Harvard University Press.

Biggadike, R. 1979. The risky business of diversification. *Harvard Business Review*, May-June: 103-111.

Blau, P. M. 1977. *Inequality and heterogeneity*. Glencoe, IL: Free Press.

Blau, P. M., & Schoenherr, R. 1971. *The structure of organizations*. New York: Basic Books.

Blunden, R. G. 1993. *Financing patterns, resource scarcity, and new venture performance*. Unpublished doctoral dissertation, The University of Western Ontario, Canada.

Bolland, E. J. 1993. *High-technology venture performance (venture capitalists)*. Unpublished doctoral dissertation, Nova University, Ft. Lauderdale.

Bollen, K. A. 1989. *Structural equations with latent variables*. New York: John Wiley & Sons.

Bollen, K. A., & Hoyle, R. H. 1990. Perceived cohesion: A conceptual and empirical examination. *Social Forces*, 69: 479-504.

Bourgeois, L. J., III. 1985. Strategic goals, perceived uncertainty, and economic performance in volatile environments. *Academy of Management Journal*, 29: 548-573.

Boyd, B. K., Dess, G. G., Rasheed, A. 1993. Divergence between archival and perceptual measures of the environment: Causes and consequences. *Academy of Management Review*, 18 (2): 204-226.

Brockhaus. R. H. 1980. Risk-taking propensity of entrepreneurs. *Academy of Management journal*, 23: 509-520.

Brush, C. G., & Vanderwerf, P. A. 1992. A comparison of methods and sources for obtaining estimates of new venture performance. *Journal of Business Venturing*, 7: 157-170.

Burns, T., & Stalker, B. M. 1961. *The management of innovation*. London: Tavistock.

Bygrave, W. D. 1989a. The entrepreneurship paradigm (I): A philosophical look at its research methodologies. *Entrepreneurship Theory and Practice*, 14 (1): 7-26.

Bygrave, W. D. 1989b. The entrepreneurship paradigm (ii): Chaos and catastrophes among quantum jumps? *Entrepreneurship Theory and Practice*, 14 (2): 7-30.

Campbell, D. T., and Fiske, D. W. 1959. Convergent and discriminant validation by the multitrait-multimethod matrix. *Psychological Bulletin*, 56 (2): 81-105.

Capon, N., Farley, J. U., & Hoenig, S. 1990. Determinants of financial performance: A meta-analysis. *Management Science*, 36 (10): 1143-1159.

Carland, J. W., & Carland, J. C. 1993. Beware the dark side of entrepreneurship: Disincentives and nostra. In Churchill, N. C., Birley, S., Bygrave, W. D., Doutriaux, J., Gatewood, E. J., Hoy, F. S., & Wetzel, Jr., W. E. (Ed.) *Frontiers of Entrepreneurship Research* (p.253). Babson Park, MA: Center for Entrepreneurial Studies, Babson College.

Carland, J. C., Hoy, F., Boulton, W. R., and Carland, J. C. 1984. Differentiating entrepreneurs from small business owners: A conceptualization. *Academy of Management Review*, 9 (2): 354-359.

Caves, R. E., & Porter, M. E. 1977. From entry barriers to mobility barriers: Conjectural decisions and contrived deterrence to new competition. *Quarterly Journal of Economics*, 91: 241-262.

Chandler, G. N., & Hanks, S. H. 1994. Founder Competence, the environment and venture performance. *Entrepreneurship: Theory and Practice*, 18 (3): 77-90.

Chandler, G. N., & Hanks, S. H. 1993. Market attractiveness, resource-based capabilities, venture strategies, and venture performance. *Journal of Business Venturing*, 9: 331-349.

Child, J. 1972. Organization structure, environment and performance: The role of strategic choice. *Sociology*, 6: 2-22.

Cohen, J. & Cohen, P. 1983. *Applied Multiple Regression/Correlation Analysis for the Behavioral Sciences*. Hillsdale, NJ: Lawrence Erlbaum Associates, Publishers.

Cooper, A. C., Willard, G. E., & Woo, C. Y. 1986. Strategies of high-performing new and small firms: A reexamination of the niche concept. *Journal of Business Venturing*, 1 (3): 247-260.

Cosier, R. A. 1978. The effects of three potential aids for making strategic decisions on prediction accuracy. *Organizational Behavior and Human Performance*, 22: 295-306.

Cosier, R. A., & Rose, G. L. 1977. Cognitive conflict and goal conflict effects on task performance. *Organizational Behavior and Human Performance*, 19: 378-391.

Cosier, R. A., & Schwenk, C. R. 1990. Agreement and thinking alike: Ingredients for poor decisions. *Academy of Management Executive*, 4: 69-74.

Covin, J.G. 1991. Entrepreneurial versus conservative firms: A comparison of strategies and performance. *Journal of Management Studies*, 28 (5): 439-463.

Covin, J.G. & Slevin, D.P. 1989. Strategic management of small firms in hostile and benign environments. *Strategic Management Journal*, 10: 75-87.

Cueto, S. 1993. *Promoting peace: Integrating curricula to deal with violence.* Paper presented at the Annual Meeting of the American Educational Research Association.

Daft, R. L. 1978. A dual-core model of organizational innovation. *Academy of Management Journal,* 21 (2): 193-210.

Dean, T. J., & Meyer, G. D. 1996. Industry environments and new venture formations in U.S. manufacturing: A conceptual and empirical analysis of demand determinants. *Journal of Business Venturing,* 11: 107-132.

Denzin, N.K. 1978. *The Research Act: A Theoretical Introduction to Sociological Methods.* New York: McGraw-Hill.

Dess, G. G., & Beard, D. W. 1984. Dimensions of organizational task environments. *Administrative Science Quarterly,* 29: 52-73.

Dess, G. G., & Davis, P. S. 1984. Porter's (1980) generic strategies as determinants of strategic group membership and organizational performance. *Academy of Management Journal,* 27: 467-488.

Dess G. G., Ireland, R. D., & Hitt, M. A. 1990. Industry effects and strategic management research. *Journal of Management,* 16 (1): 7-27.

Dess, G. G., & Rasheed A. 1991. Conceptualizing and measuring organizational environments: a critique and suggestions. *Journal of Management,* 17 (4): 701-710.

Dillman, D. A. 1978. *Mail and telephone surveys: The total design method.* New York: John Wiley and Sons.

Drucker, P. F. 1985. *Innovation and Entrepreneurship.* New York: Harper and Row.

Duncan, R. G. 1972. Characteristics of organizational task environments. *Administrative Science Quarterly,* 17: 313-327.

Edwards, P. K., & Scullion, H. 1982. *The social organization of industrial conflict.* Oxford: Basil Blackwell.

Ensley, M. D., & Banks, M. C. 1992. *Raising questions about entrepreneurial teams.* In the proceedings of the 1992 meeting of the Southern Management Association.

Eisenhardt, K. 1989. Making fast strategic decisions in high-velocity environments. *Academy of Management Journal,* 32 (3): 543-576.

Eisenhardt, K. M., & Bourgeois, L. J. 1988. Politics of strategic decision making in high-velocity environments: Toward a midrange theory. *Academy of Management Journal,* 31 (4): 737-770.

Eisenhardt, K., & Schoonhoven, C. B. 1990. Organizational growth: Linking founding team, strategy, environment, and growth among U. S. semiconductor ventures, 1978- 1988. *Administrative Science Quarterly,* 35: 504-529.

Festinger, L. 1950. Informal social communication. *Psychological Review*, 57: 271- 292.

Fredrickson, J. W. 1984. The comprehensiveness of strategic decision processes: Extension, observations, and future directions. *Academy of Management Journal*, 27: 445-466.

Fredrickson, J. W., & Mitchell, T. R. 1984. Strategic decision processes: Comprehensiveness and performance in an industry with an unstable environment. *Academy of Management Journal*, 27: 399-423.

Gartner, W.B. 1988. "Who is an entrepreneur?" is the wrong question. *American Journal of Small Business*, 12(4), 11-32.

Gartner, W. B. 1985. A conceptual framework for describing new venture formation. *Academy of Management Review*, 10 (4): 696-706.

Gartner, W. B., Bird, B. J., & Starr, J. A. 1992. Acting as if: Differentiating entrepreneurial from organizational behavior. *Entrepreneurship: Theory and Practice*, 16 (3): 13-31.

Gartner, W. B., Shaver, K. G., Gatewood, E., & Katz, J. A. 1994. Finding the entrepreneur in entrepreneurship. *Entrepreneurship: Theory and Practice*, 18 (3): 5-10.

Ginsberg, A. 1984. Operationalizing organizational strategy: Toward an integrative framework. *Academy of Management Review*, 9: 548-557.

Gladstein, D. 1984. A model of task group effectiveness. *Administrative Science Quarterly*, 29 (4): 499-517.

Goodman, P. S., Ravlin, E., & Schminke, M. 1987. Understanding groups in organizations. In L. L. Cummings and B. M. Staw. (Eds.). *Research in Organizational Behavior*, 9: 121-173. Greenwich, CT: JAI Press.

Grinyer, P. H., & Yasai-Ardekani, M. 1981. Strategy, structure, size, and bureaucracy. *Academy of Management Journal*, 24: 471-486.

Hair, Jr., J. F., Anderson, R. E., Tatham, R. L., & Black, W. C. 1995. *Multivariate Data Analysis with Readings*. Englewood Cliffs, NJ: Prentice Hall.

Hall, H. J. 1989. *Venture capitalists' decision-making and the entrepreneur: An exploratory investigation*. Unpublished doctoral dissertation, University of Georgia, Athens.

Hambrick, D. C. 1993. Top management groups: A conceptual integration and reconsideration of the "team" label. In L. L. Cummings and B. M. Staw. (Eds.) *Research in Organizational Behavior*, Greenwich, CT: JAI Press.

Hambrick, D. C., & Snow, C. C. 1977. A contextual model of strategic decision making in organizations. *Proceedings of the Academy of Management*, : 109-112.

Harrigan, K. R. 1981. Barriers to entry and competitive strategies. *Strategic Management Journal*, 2: 395-412.

Harrison, A. W. 1993. *Work-group effectiveness: A structural equations analysis of the effects of individual differences.* Unpublished doctoral dissertation, Auburn University, Auburn.

Herron, L. 1990. *The effects of characteristics of the entrepreneur on new venture performance.* Unpublished doctoral dissertation, University of South Carolina, Columbia, S.C.

Hinitz, B. 1995. Educating young children for peace. *ERS - Spectrum*, 13 (4): 22-27.

Hobson, E. L., & Morrison, R. M. 1983. How do corporate start-up ventures fare? *Frontiers of Entrepreneurship Research.* Wellesley: Babson College.

Hofer, C. W., & Schendel, D. 1978. *Strategy formulation: Analytical concepts.* St. Paul: West Publishing.

Hogg, M. 1987. Social identity and group cohesiveness. In Turner, J. C. (Ed.). *Rediscovering the Social Group: A Self-Categorization Theory*: 89-116.

Jackson, S. E., Brett, J. F., Sessa, V. I., Cooper, D. M., Julin, J. A., & Peyronnin, K. 1991. Some differences make a difference: Individual dissimilarity and group heterogeneity as correlates of recruitment, promotion and turnover. *Journal of Applied Psychology*, 79 (5): 675-689.

Jehn, K. A. 1992. *The impact of intragroup conflict on effectiveness: A multi-method examination of the benefits and detriments of conflict.* Unpublished doctoral dissertation, Northwestern University, Evanston, IL.

Jenssen, S. A. 1991. *New venture formation and success: Factors influencing the supply and subsequent success of new ventures.* Unpublished doctoral dissertation, Norges Tekniske Hogskole, Norway.

Jurkovich, R. 1972. A core typology of organizational environments. *Administrative Science Quarterly*, 380-394.

Kabanoff, B. 1991. Equity, equality, power, and conflict. *Academy of Management Review*, 16(2): 416-441.

Kamm, J. B. & Nurick, A. J. 1993. The stages of team venture formation: A decision- making model. *Entrepreneurship Theory and Practice*, 17 (2): 17-28.

Kamm, J. B., Shuman, J. C., Seeger, J. A., & Nurick, A. J. 1990. Entrepreneurial teams in new venture creation: A research agenda. *Entrepreneurship Theory and Practice*, 14 (4): 7-17.

Katz, J. A., & Gartner, W. B. 1988. Properties of emerging organization. *Academy of Management Review*, 13 (3): 429-441.

Katz, R. L. 1974. Skills of an effective administrator. *Harvard Business Review*, 52 (5): 90-102.

Keats, B. W., & Hitt, M. A. 1988. A causal model of linkages among environmental dimensions, macro organizational characteristics, and performance. *Academy of Management Journal*, 31: 570-598.

Khandwalla, P. N. Winter 1976/1977. Some top management styles, their context and performance. *Organization and Administrative Sciences*, 7 (4): 21-51.

Kirzner, I. M. 1979. *Perception, opportunity, and profit: Studies in the theory of entrepreneurship.* Chicago: University of Chicago Press.

Klein, B. 1977. *Dynamic economics.* Cambridge, MA: Harvard University Press.

Kunkel, S. W. 1991. *The impact of strategy and industry structure on new venture performance.* Unpublished doctoral dissertation, University of Georgia, Athens.

Lawless, M. W., & Finch, L. K. 1989. Choice and determinism: A test of Hrebiniak and Joyce's framework on strategy-environment fit. *Strategic Management Journal*, 10: 351-365.

Lawrence, P. R., & Lorsch, J. 1969. *Organization and environment.* Homewood, Ill.: Richard D. Irwin.

Loehlin, J. C. 1992. *Latent variable models: An introduction to factor, path, and structural analysis.* Hillsdale, NJ: Lawrence Erlbaum Associates.

Lumpkin, G. T., & Dess, G. G. 1996. Clarifying the entrepreneurial orientation construct and linking it to performance. *Academy of Management Review*, 21(1): 135- 172.

MacMillan, I. C., & Day, D. L. 1987. Corporate ventures into industrial markets: Dynamics of aggressive entry. *Journal of Business Venturing*, 2 (1): 29-39.

McArthur A. W., Nystrom, P. C. 1991. Environmental dynamism, complexity, and munificence as moderators of strategy-performance relationships. *Journal of Business Research*, 23 : 349-361.

McCarthy, A. M. 1992. *The role of strategy, environment, resources, and strategic change in new venture performance.* Unpublished doctoral dissertation, Purdue University, Lafayette.

McDougall, P. 1987. *An analysis of new venture business level strategy, entry barriers, and new venture origin as factors explaining new venture performance.* Unpublished doctoral dissertation, University of South Carolina, Columbia.

McDougall, P., Robinson, Jr., R., DeNisi, A. 1992. Modeling new venture performance: An analysis of new venture strategy, industry structure, and venture origin. *Journal of Business Venturing*, 7: 267-289.

McGuire, J., Schneeweis, T., & Hill, J. 1986. An analysis of alternative measures of strategic performance. In *Advances in Strategic Management*: 124-156, New York: JAI Press.

Merz, G. R., & Sauber, M. H. 1995. Profiles of managerial activities in small firms. *Strategic Management Journal*, 16 (7): 551-564.

Michel, J., & Hambrick D. C. 1992. Diversification posture and top management team characteristics. *Academy of Management Journal*, 35: 9-37.

Miller, D. 1993. The architecture of simplicity. *Academy of Management Review*, 18 (1): 116-138.

Miller, D. 1990. *The Icarus Paradox: How exceptional companies bring about their own downfall: new lessons in the dynamics of corporate success, decline, and renewal*. Greenfield, CT: Harper Collins.

Miller, D. 1988. Relating Porter's business strategies to environment and structure: Analysis and performance implications. *Academy of Management Journal*, 31: 280- 308.

Miller, D. 1983. The correlates of entrepreneurship in three types of firms. *Management Science*, 29: 770-791.

Miller, A., & Camp, B. 1985. Exploring determents of success in corporate ventures. *Journal of Business Venturing*, 1: 87-105.

Miller, D., & Friesen, P. H. 1984. *Organizations: A Quantum View*. Englewood Cliffs, NJ: Prentice Hall.

Miller, D., & Friesen, P. H. 1983. Strategy-making and environment: The third link. *Strategic Management Journal*, 4: 221-235.

Miller, D., & Friesen, P. H. 1982. Innovation in conservative and entrepreneurial firms: Two models of strategic momentum. *Strategic Management Journal*, 3: 1-25.

Mintzberg, H. 1973. Strategy making in three modes. *California Management Review*, 16 (2): 44-53.

Mintzberg, H. 1979. *The structuring of organizations*. Englewood Cliffs, NJ: Prentice- Hall.

Mintzberg, H. 1983. Why America needs, but cannot have, corporate democracy. *Organizational Dynamics*, 11(4): 5-20.

Mintzberg, H. 1987. Crafting Strategy. *Harvard Business Review*, July-August: 66-75.

Mintzberg, H. 1994. The Fall and Rise of Strategic Planning. *Harvard Business Review*, January-February: 107-114.

Murray, A. I. 1989. Top management group heterogeneity and firm performance. *Strategic Management Journal*, 10: 125-141.

Naman, J. L., & Slevin, D. P. 1993. Entrepreneurship and the concept of fit: A model and empirical tests. *Strategic Management Journal*, 14: 137-153.

Neter, J., Wasserman, W., & Kutner, M. H. 1990. *Applied Linear Statistical Models*. Homewood, IL: Irwin, Inc.

Norburn, D., & Birley, S. 1988. The top management team and corporate performance. *Strategic Management Journal*, 9: 225-237.

Nunnally, J. C., & Bernstein, I. H. 1994. *Psychometric theory* (3rd ed.). New York: McGraw-Hill.

Nwachukwu, O. C, & Tsalikis, J. 1989. Environmental heterogeneity, strategy-making, structure and small business performance: A path analytic model. *The Journal of Applied Business Research*, 7 (2): 38-44.

Pfeffer, J. 1983. Organizational demography. *Research in Organization Behavior*, 5: 299-357.

Pfeffer J., & Salancik G. R. 1978. *The external control of organizations: A resource dependence perspective.* New York: Harper and Row.

Porter, M. E. 1980. *Competitive strategy: Techniques for analyzing industries and competitors.* New York: Free Press.

Prescott, J. 1986. Environments as moderators of the relationship between strategy and performance. *Academy of Management Journal*, 29: 329-346.

Robinson, K. C. 1995. *Measures of entrepreneurial value creation: An investigation of the impact of strategy and industry structure on the economic performance of independent new ventures.* Unpublished doctoral dissertation, University of Georgia, Athens.

Romanelli, E. 1987. New venture strategies in the minicomputer industry. *California Management Review*, 30 (1): 160-175.

Roure, J. B., & Maidique, M. A. 1986. Linking prefunding factors and high-technology venture success: An exploratory study. *Journal of Business Venturing*, 1 (3): 295-306.

Rumelt, R. P. 1986. *Strategy, structure, and economic performance.* Boston: Harvard Business School Press.

Sandberg, W. R. 1986. *New venture performance: The role of strategy and industry structure.* Lexington, MA: D. C. Heath and Co.

Schaefer, A. D., Kenny, J. T., & Bost, J. E. 1990. Performance measures and strategy: A review, critique, and extension. *Advances in Marketing*: 152-157.

Schein, E. H. 1985. *Organizational culture.* San Francisco: Jossey-Bass.

Schumpeter, J. 1942. *Capitalism, socialism, and democracy.* New York: Harper & Row.

Schweiger, D. M., Sandberg, W. R. & Rechner, P. L. 1989. Experiential effects of dialectical inquiry, devil's advocacy, and consensus approaches to strategic decision making. *Academy of Management Journal*, 32: 745-772.

Schweiger, D. M., Sandberg, W. R. & Ragan, J. W. 1986. Group approaches for improving strategic decision making: A comparative analysis of dialectical inquiry, devil's advocacy, and consensus. *Academy of Management Journal*, 29: 51-71.

Seashore, S. E. 1954. *Group cohesiveness in the industrial work group.* Ann Arbor: University of Michigan Press.

Sharfman, M., & Dean, J., Jr. 1991. Conceptualizing and measuring the organizational environment: A multidimensional approach. *Journal of Management*, 17 (4): 681-700.

Siegel, R., Siegel, E., & MacMillan, I. C. 1993. Characteristics distinguishing high-growth ventures. *Journal of Business Venturing*, 8 (2): 169-180.

Snyder, N. H., & Glueck, W. F. 1982. Can environmental volatility be measured objectively? *Academy of Management Journal*, 25 (1): 185-192.

Staw, B. M., Sandelands, L. E., & Dutton, J. E. 1981. Threat-rigidity effects in organizational behavior: A multilevel analysis. *Administrative Science Quarterly*, 26: 501-524.

Stearns, T., Carter, N., Reynolds, P., & Williams, M. 1995. New firm survival: Industry, strategy, and location. *Journal of Business Venturing*, 10: 23-42.

Stuart, R., & Abetti, P. A. 1987. Start-up ventures: Towards the prediction of initial success. *Journal of Business Venturing*, 2: 215-230.

Szilagyi, A. D., & Schweiger, D. M. 1984. Matching managers to strategies: A review and suggested framework. *Academy of Management Review*, 9 (4): 626-637.

Tan, J.J & Litschert, R.J. (1994) Environment-strategy relationship and its performance implications: an empirical study of the Chinese electronics industry. *Strategic Management Journal*, 15(1): 1-20.

Thompson, J. D. 1967. *Organizations in action.* New York: McGraw-Hill Book Co.

Tosi, H., Aldag, R., & Storey, R. 1973. On the measurement of the environment: An assessment of the Lawrence and Lorsch environmental subscale. *Administrative Science Quarterly*, 18: 27-36.

Venkatraman, N. & Grant, J.H. 1986. Construct measurement in strategy research: A critique and proposal. *Academy of Management Journal.*, 11, 71-86.

Venkatraman, N. 1989. Strategic orientation of business enterprises: The construct, dimensionality, and measurement. *Management Science*, 35 (8): 942-967.

Vesper, K. H. 1990. *New Venture Strategies* (revised edition). Englewood Cliffs, N.J.: Prentice Hall.

Virany, B., & Tushman, M. L. 1986. Top management teams and corporate success in an emerging industry. *Journal of Business Venturing*, 1: 261-274.

Von Hippel, E. 1977. Successful and failing internal corporate ventures: An empirical analysis. *Industrial Marketing Management*, 6: 163-173.

Wagner, W. G., Pfeffer, J., & O'Reilly, C. A. 1984. Organizational demography and turnover in top-management groups. *Administrative Science Quarterly*, 29: 74-92.

Weick, K. E. 1979. *The Social Psychology of Organizing* (2d ed.). New York: Random House.

West, P., & Meyer, D. 1994. *The relationship between performance and consensus among top managers in entrepreneurial firms.* Paper presented at the 1994 State of Entrepreneurship Conference, Babson, PA.

White, H. 1980. A heteroskedasticity-consistent covariance matrix estimator and a direct test for heteroskedastcicty. *Econometrica*, 48: 817-838.

Wholey, D. R., Brittain, J. 1989. Characterizing environmental variation. *Academy of Management Journal*, 32 (4): 867-882.

Wiersema, M. & Bantel, K. 1992. Top management team demography and corporate strategic change. *Academy of Management Journal*, 35: 91-121.

Wiersema, M., & Bird, A. 1993. Organizational demography in Japanese firms: Group heterogeneity, individual dissimilarity, and top management team turnover. *Academy of Management Journal*, 36 (5): 996-1025.

Yip, G. S. 1982. *Barriers to Entry*. Lexington, MA: Lexington Books.

Zahra, S. A., & Covin, J. G. 1993. Business strategy, technology policy and firm performance. *Strategic Management Journal*, 14: 451-478.

Compustat Database

Small Business Administration, 1994. *The state of small business: A report to the President.* Washington D.C.: United States Government Printing Office.

U.S. Bureau of the Census. 1992. Census of Manufacturers. Washington D.C.: U.S. Government Printing Office.

U.S. Bureau of the Census. 1995. Annual Survey of Manufacturers. Washington D.C.: U.S. Government Printing Office.

U.S. Bureau of the Census. 1995. Annual Service Survey. Washington D.C.: U.S. Government Printing Office.

U.S. Bureau of the Census. 1983-1993. County Business Patterns. Washington D.C.: U.S. Government Printing Office.

U.S. Bureau of Labor Statistics. 1994-1995. Employment Hours and Earnings. Washington D.C.: U.S. Government Printing Office.

U.S. Bureau of the Census. 1995. Census of Service Industries. Washington D.C.: U.S. Government Printing Office.

U.S. Bureau of the Census. 1992. Census of Wholesale Trade. Washington D.C.: U.S. Government Printing Office.

U.S. Bureau of the Census. 1992. Census of Retail Trade. Washington D.C.: U.S. Government Printing Office.

U.S. Bureau of the Census. 1992. Census of Construction. Washington D.C.: U.S. Government Printing Office.

U.S. Bureau of the Census. 1996. Annual Wholesale and Retail Summary. Washington D.C.: U.S. Government Printing Office.

U.S. Bureau of the Census. 1985-1994. Annual Construction Survey. Washington D.C.: U.S. Government Printing Office.

U.S. Bureau of the Census. 1992. Census of Transportation. Washington D.C.: U.S. Government Printing Office.

U.S. Bureau of the Census. 1993. Motor Freight Transportation and Warehousing Survey. Washington, D.C.: U.S. Government Printing Office.

U.S. Bureau of the Census. 1994. Annual Survey of Communications Industry. Washington, D.C.: U.S. Government Printing Office.

U.S. Bureau of the Census. 1991, and 1995. The Statistical Abstract of the U.S. Washington D.C.: U.S. Government Printing Office.

National Science Foundation. 1996. Science and Engineering Indicators. Washington D.C.: U.S. Government Printing Office.

U.S. Bureau of the Census. 1993. County Business Patterns. Washington D.C.: U.S. Government Printing Office.

U. S. Bureau of the Census. 1991. Industry Classification Manual. Washington D.C.: U.S. Government Printing Office.

Ward's Business Directory, Vol. 5. 1990, 1993, & 1996. Detroit, MI: Gale Publishing.

Dun & Bradstreet's Market Indentifiers Database. 1994.

# Author Index

Dean, J., Jr., 5, 11, 39, 46, 47, 55–59, 61, 96
Dean, T. J., 96
DeNisi, A., 6
Denzin, N. K., 43
Dess, G. G., 5, 11, 32, 35, 36–38, 47, 53–56, 58, 59, 94, 97, 100
Dillman, D. A., 48, 64
Drucker, P. F., 4, 37
Duncan, R. G., 46, 47, 54, 94

Edwards, P. K., 44
Eisenhardt, K. M., 13, 23, 26–29, 30–32
Ensley, M. D., 4, 8, 43, 47, 96

Festinger, L., 21
Finch, L. K., 55
Fiske, D. W. , 43
Friesen, P. H., 2, 5, 9–11, 31, 32, 34, 35, 38, 39, 41, 45, 46, 50, 53, 54, 95, 100

Gartner W.B., 1–3, 5–9, 22, 24, 43, 48, 92, 97, 100
Gatewood, E. J., 1, 92
Ginsberg, A., 97, 99, 100
Gladstein, D., 12, 21, 99
Glueck, W. F., 54, 56, 94
Goodman, P. S., 21
Grinyer, P. H., 40

Hair, Jr., 66, 70
Hambrick D. C., 12, 18, 21, 25, 44
Hanks, S. H., 7, 35, 47, 59
Harrigan, K. R., 11
Harrison, A. W., 20–23, 50, 51
Herron, L., 4, 7, 48, 49, 61, 92
Hill, J., 59
Hinitz, B., 9
Hitt, M. A., 11, 36, 38, 40, 54, 55, 59, 94, 96

Hobson, E. L., 97
Hofer, C. W., 40
Hogg, M., 21, 22
Hoy, F. S., 1
Hoyle, R. H., 21

Ireland, R. D., 11, 36, 54, 55, 94

Jackson, S. E., 12, 19–24, 44, 50, 61, 72
Jehn, K. A., 4, 9, 31, 44, 50
Jurkovich, R., 47

Kabanoff, B., 12, 21, 23, 25, 26, 31, 32
Kamm, J. B., 4, 8, 22, 24, 43, 48
Katz, J. A., 1, 6, 92
Katz, R. L., 4, 48, 72
Keats, B. W., 38, 40, 55, 59, 96
Kenny, G. T., 59
Khandwalla, P. N., 39
Kirzner, I. M., 3
Klein, B., 58
Kuh, E., 61, 71
Kunkel, S. W., 93, 95, 97
Kutner, M. H., 71

Lawless, M. W., 55
Lawrence, P. R., 40, 46
Litschert, R.J., 34
Loehlin, J. C., 66
Lorsch, J., 40, 46
Lumpkin, G. T., 35, 53, 97, 100

MacMillan, I. C., 22, 93
Maidique, M. A., 4, 9, 22, 24, 48
McArthur A. W., 38, 55
McDougall, P., 6, 7, 10, 11, 14, 18, 33, 35–37, 39–41, 53, 83, 92–94, 97
McGuire, J., 59
Merz, G. R., 11
Meyer, D., 28–31, 96

# Subject Index

affective conflict, 6, 12–13, 18–21,
  23–24, 27–29, 32–34, 36–39,
  43–45, 59, 61–62, 65, 68,
  70–71, 86, 94, 96, 100–107,
  120, 131, 179–183
aggressiveness, 6, 46, 63, 72, 74,
  93, 96, 104, 108–111, 114–116,
  118, 120, 130, 172–177,
  179–183
analysis, 7, 58, 63–64, 70, 72–74,
  76, 83–85, 88–89, 91–93,
  95–99, 100, 104–105,
  108–110, 114–116, 120,
  130–131, 133, 139–140, 142,
  144–145, 147–148, 156, 161,
  167, 172–177, 179–183

business strategy, 5, 8–10, 45, 149

cognitive conflict, 6, 12–14, 17,
  19–20, 23–24, 26, 29, 33–44,
  61–62, 70–71, 86, 94, 96, 100,
  102–104, 120, 122–124, 131,
  140, 154, 179–183
competitive threat, 7, 56, 58–59,
  65–66, 81–82, 112–113, 117,

120, 126, 158, 167, 175–177,
  179–183
complexity, 7, 33, 52, 54, 58–59,
  65, 76, 80–81, 112–113, 117,
  120, 126, 134, 144, 158, 168,
  172–174, 178–183

defensiveness, 46, 72, 93–97,
  108–111, 114–116, 120, 130,
  156, 172–177, 179
devil's advocacy, 34–36, 147
dialectical inquiry, 35–36, 147
dynamism, 7, 52, 54–56, 58–59,
  65, 75–76, 79–81, 112–116,
  118, 120, 126, 128, 131, 144,
  158, 166, 179–183

entrepreneur, 1–2, 5, 8–11, 14, 39,
  66, 83, 88–90, 122, 124–125,
  128, 132, 135, 138–139,
  141–142, 152, 162–164
entrepreneurial firms, 1–2, 4–6,
  12–13, 15, 19, 21, 31–32,
  38–39, 41, 45–48, 63, 66, 83,
  107, 117, 126, 128, 145, 149,
  160, 162–164

*159*